Chinese Takeout Cookbook

Easy Recipes to Make at Home

Maylin Sun

CONTENTS

INTRODUCTION

Want to order Asian takeout but don't want to wait 40 minutes for delivery? You've obviously chosen the correct book and are in the right place. The most popular takeaway meals (beef and broccoli, I'm looking at you!), cozy noodles and rice, Asian seafood dishes, Chinese dim sum, soups and stews, and more are all included in our finest imitation Chinese takeout recipes that you can cook at home now. Making takeout meals at home is furthermore quicker, tastier, and healthier than ordering food from a restaurant. Yes, the majority of these recipes can be prepared in under 30 minutes.

Take a minute to relax and picture biting into a hot, flavorful egg roll. Or a flavorful pork dumpling. Alternatively, a fiery bite of General Tso's chicken. Even if the tastes of different foods vary, chances are we're all picturing the same emotion: pleasure.

Chinese takeout is a food that is quite American in many aspects. Many of us consumed just as much Chinese cuisine as hamburgers and hot dogs as children. From potlucks to poker nights, from late-night study sessions to cross-country road journeys, comfort food has supported many occasions.

Chinese restaurants may be found anywhere, whether you're in Brooklyn, Bozeman, or Biloxi. If you reside in a city, there's a good possibility that your kitchen drawers are overflowing with disposable chopsticks, soy sauce packets, and takeaway menus.

Most of the regional Chinese cuisines that we presently enjoy, such as Sichuan, Hunan, and Fujianese, precede the introduction of American-style Chinese food. The first Chinese eateries in the country were established in California during the gold rush in the late 1840s and early 1850s by Cantonese immigrants who were discriminated against and had difficulty getting employment on the railways. The majority of chefs learned how to cook by recreating dishes from their own homes using items they discovered in this strange new environment. Chinese and non-Chinese employees were served by restaurants in the mining towns; the food was inexpensive and served in huge servings. Urban sophisticates were drawn to San Francisco's more affluent restaurants because they were interested in the "strange" foods and wanted to tell their friends about them. Restaurants accompanied the migration of railroad employees, both Chinese and non-Chinese, and prospered, particularly in urban areas.

Popular Chinese cuisine had entered the cultural lexicon by the early 20th century. In his 1929 picture Chop Suey, artist Edward Hopper depicts two ladies idling in a Chinese restaurant while sipping tea. Sinclair Lewis explains how the main heroine of his 1920s Minnesota book Main Street, a city girl, strives to bring chow mein and other Chinese dishes to her outlying neighbors. Egg foo young is also mentioned by poet Carl Sandburg in his epic poem "The People, Yes," published in 1936. Chinese takeaway and eateries have been embedded in the lives of the characters in recent episodes of hit television programs like Seinfeld and Sex and the City. Chinese eateries had evolved into hip hangouts for young urbanites by the middle of the 20th century. You could have chow mein or fried rice at the Cotton Club in New York in addition to your gin fizz. A whole eating experience was built around pupu platters of egg rolls, barbecued ribs, and wontons in tiki restaurants in California, led by the Trader Vic's chain and Don the Beachcomber, with mai tais and Singapore slings to wash it all down. The idea of Chinese meal delivery became viral in Manhattan in the 1970s.

Chinese eateries and the concept of takeaway quickly migrated to the suburbs and small towns and established themselves as a staple of millions of Americans' everyday lives. In the United States, there are already over 40,000 Chinese restaurants, and new ones are emerging daily. Some have even turned their adaptations of Chinese cuisine into well-known regional specialties: in Hawaii, you may buy kalua pig steamed buns. In Rhode Island, chow mein sandwiches. And in Louisiana, soy vinegar crawfish. What was first considered foreign in this nation has been completely Americanized.

Although Americanized Chinese cuisine is a natural byproduct of Chinese immigration, it may be just as delicious as food found on the Chinese mainland. Since all cuisines have developed from someplace, whether it is Cajun food, Italian food (tomato sauce was nonexistent in Italy until the late 1600s), American-Chinese food, or even Chinese food in China, I try to avoid using the term "genuine" wherever possible. Across provinces, nations, and continents, food nearly always has to vary and adapt in order to employ regional ingredients and satisfy regional preferences. If a chef has to change a recipe, it's not a scandal as long as they do it carefully and expertly. We wouldn't have deep-dish pizza, hamburgers, baked ziti, jambalaya, or many more American classic dishes without a cross-cultural fusion of cuisines. The American tale also gave rise to American-Chinese staples like chow mein and shrimp in lobster sauce, all of which are wonderful when prepared properly.

COPYCAT TAKEOUT EGG ROLLS

PREP: 1 hour 30 minutes

COOK: 30 minutes

Ingredients

- 8 cups of savory cabbage
- 8 cups of green cabbage
- 2 cups of carrot
- 2 cups of celery
- 3 scallions
- 2 1/2 tsp salt
- 2 tsp sugar
- 1 tbsp sesame oil
- 2 tbsp peanut or vegetable oil
- 1/4 tsp five spice powder (optional)
- 1/4 tsp white pepper
- 3 cups of roast pork
- 2 cups of cooked shrimp
- 1 package egg roll wrappers
- 1 egg

Instructions

1. Bring a lot of water to a boil in a big saucepan. Boiling water should be used to cook the cabbage, carrots, and celery for around two minutes. Place the vegetables in an ice bath and then drain them. Squeeze the vegetables well to remove all of the extra water.This is a crucial step

because if the filling is too moist, the egg rolls will turn out to be soggy.

2. Take the vegetables in a large mixing bowl when they have dried. Add the white pepper, roast pork, cooked shrimp, scallions, salt, sugar, sesame oil, and 2 tbsp of oil (if using). Throw everything into the mix. The filling is prepared for wrapping!

3. To wrap the egg rolls, take a tiny amount of filling, compress it in your fingers slightly, and then lay it on the wrapper. Burrito-style wrapping is used in this process. To ensure that it remains sealed, just add a thin coating of egg. Up until you run out of ingredients, arrange them in a line on a surface that has been gently dusted with flour.

4. Heat the oil in a saucepan to 325 degrees. Just enough to cover the egg rolls is all that is required. A few egg rolls should be carefully placed into the oil and fried for about 5 minutes or until golden brown. To ensure even frying, keep them moving in the oil.

5. Once somewhat chilled, serve! Then, reheat them in the oven at 350degree F until crispy. Freeze leftovers in freezer bags.

VEGETABLE AND PORK SPRING ROLLS

Prep Time: 40 minutes

Cook Time: 25 minutes

Ingredients

Filling

- 1 cup of sliced bamboo shoots, about 4 ounces
- 2 tbsp peanut oil, divided
- 6 ounces ground pork
- 1/3 cup of diced shallots, about 1/2 of a large shallot
- 1 3/4 cups of shredded carrots, about 5 ounces
- 3 cups of chopped green cabbage, about 7.5 ounces
- 1/2 cup of diced water chestnuts
- 1 tbsp cornstarch
- 2 tbsp water
- 1 tbsp oyster sauce
- 1 tsp salt
- 1 tsp sugar
- 1/2 tsp ground white pepper

Spring Rolls

- 15-20 8-inch spring roll wrappers-
- 1 egg, lightly beaten
- oil for frying

To Serve

- sweet chili sauce

Instructions

Prepare the Filling

1. In the saucepan, bring a few glasses of water to a boil. The bamboo shoots should be added and blanched for 1 minute to remove the smell. With cold water, drain and rinse.

2. In a wok over high heat, warm 1 tbsp of peanut oil. Cook for two to three minutes after adding the meat. The pork does not have to be totally cooked, but the exterior should start to become white. To cut the meat into little pieces, use the end of your spatula. Put the meat on a platter.

3. Incorporate the wok with the last tbsp of peanut oil. After adding, saute the shallots for approximately a minute. Cook for 2 minutes after adding the water chestnuts, bamboo shoots, cabbage, carrots, and bamboo. Add the meat back into the pan after that and stir.

4. Combine the cornstarch and water in a small bowl to create a slurry. To make room at the bottom of the pan, use your spatula to push the pork and veggies to the side. Fill the gap with the cornstarch slurry. Allow the slurry to thicken for 30 seconds before stirring it into the other ingredients.

5. White pepper, salt, sugar, and oyster sauce should all be added. Stir the ingredients and spices together. For a 10-minute cooling period, spread the filling out on a large baking sheet. Never pour any liquid onto a baking sheet. You shouldn't use the hot filling to wrap your spring rolls. The spring roll wrappers will get soggy due to the heat, making rolling the spring rolls challenging. The wrapping may also become readily disintegrated as a result.

6. Place the Spring Roll-Making Station in place.

7. The wrappers for spring rolls are simple to dry. I typically remove a small stack of wrappers from the box at a time (around 5 or 6). Then, to keep them from drying out, cover the wrappers with a thick, dry towel. It may also be wrapped with plastic.

8. Prepare a large baking sheet or a number of sizable dishes so that you can arrange the spring rolls on top after they have been folded up. Be careful to have a dry towel close by to cover the spring rolls after they are folded up.

9. Put the egg wash and filling close by.

10. the spring rolls in advance (refer to photos in the post for visuals)

11. Take one spring roll wrapper sheet, and lay it out on the counter in the form of a diamond with one corner pointing in your direction. Put roughly 2 tsp of the filling in the bottom. My preferred spacing between the filler and the bottom corner is between 1.5 and 2 inches.

12. Grab the bottom corner of the spring roll and begin rolling it up. When you revery the middle of the wrapping, halt. Fold the wrapper's left and right edges toward the center. Egg wash should be applied with the brush to the top corner. Completely fold up the spring roll. Put the spring roll on the baking sheet, wrap it up, and cover it with a dry cloth.

13. Use the remaining wrappers and filling to complete the same.

Cook the Spring Rolls

1. Over 2 big plates or a baking sheet, spread paper towels. Your spring rolls will be drained over these paper towels.

2. 2 inches of oil should be added to the wok (measured from the bottom of the wok). For many minutes, heat the oil at a medium- high temperature. You may notice little bubbles quickly bubbling around the chopstick if you stick a bamboo or wooden chopstick into the wok's bottom. That indicates that the oil is hot enough to cook (see note 5).

3. 5 spring rolls should be carefully lowered into the heated oil along the wok's edge. This lessens the chance of hot oil splattering. Fry the spring rolls for 3 to 4 minutes, turning them halfway through to ensure an even browning. Use a kitchen spider or a skimmer to remove the spring rolls from the wok once they are golden brown.

4. As the oil is still heating up, the first batch normally takes a bit longer. Reduce the heat a little if you find that the spring rolls are browning fast (becoming dark brown in about a minute).

5. Fry the remaining spring rolls until done, then turn off the heat.

6. Serve the spring rolls with sweet chili sauce right away.

VEGETARIAN SPRING ROLLS

Prep:35 minutes

Cook:30 minutes

Ingredients

- 1 nest of vermicelli rice noodles
- 1 Chinese finely shredded leaf cabbage
- 2 carrots peeled
- 150g beansprouts
- 3 spring onions, thinly sliced
- 1 tbsp sesame oil
- 2 tbsp soy sauce
- 2 tbsp Shaoxing wine
- 15g finely chopped coriande
- 1 pack of spring roll wrappers
- 1.5l vegetable oil for frying

For a spicy dipping sauce

- 2 tbsp soy sauce
- ½ - 1 tsp crispy chili and garlic oil
- 2 tbsp rice vinegar
- 1 spring onion, finely sliced

Instructions

1. Rice noodles should be drained after 15 minutes of soaking in cold water to make them more flexible. A big bowl should be filled with cabbage, carrots, bean sprouts, and spring onion whites. The cabbage combination is added to the heated sesame oil in a big pan. Cook the cabbage for 1-2 minutes over high heat or until it has just begun to wilt. Squeeze in the Shaoxing wine and soy sauce. Add the drained noodles, coriander, and the green

sections of the spring onion after cooking for a brief while until the liquid has somewhat decreased. Mix everything thoroughly to make sure it is equally coated. Spread out to cool somewhat on a platter after transfer.

2. Set a spring roll wrapper in the shape of a diamond on your work surface when the mixture has somewhat cooled. In the center of the pastry, form a sausage shape using a heaping spoonful. The pastry's top corner should be folded over the bottom corner, which should be raised. Roll the pastry into form, being sure to tuck the ends inside as you bring the pastry from the left side over the filling. By using a little water, the last corner is sealed.

3. Making sure the pan is no more than two-thirds full, heat the vegetable oil in a big, deep pan to 180C. 4-5 minutes, in batches, until golden brown, cook the spring rolls. The spring roll wrapper will sizzle when it is cooked if you put a small amount of it into the oil without a thermometer. In the meantime, carry on frying and transfer to a baking sheet to keep warm in a low oven. In a bowl, mix all the ingredients for the hot dipping sauce, taste it, and, if desired, add more chili oil. Give the spring rolls a spicy dipping sauce or some sweet chili sauce.

FRIED WONTON RECIPE

Prep Time: 45 minutes

Cook time: 15 minutes

Ingredients

- 1 pound ground pork
- 1/2 cup of shiitake mushrooms finely minced
- 1/4 cup of green onions thinly sliced
- 1 tbsp soy sauce
- 1 tsp toasted sesame oil
- 1 tsp cornstarch
- 1/2 tsp salt
- 1/4 tsp pepper
- 1/2 tsp minced ginger
- 1 tsp minced garlic
- 12-ounce package square wonton wrappers vegetable oil for frying
- sweet chili sauce for serving optional

Instructions

1. Mix the pork, mushrooms, green onions, soy sauce, sesame oil, cornstarch, salt, pepper, ginger, and garlic together in a large bowl. Mix all ingredients by stirring them together.

2. Spread out a single wonton wrapper. Cover the remaining wrappers to prevent them from drying out. Brush water down the two corners of the wonton wrapper that are not closest to you.

3. In the middle of the wrapper, place 3/4 of a tsp of the pork filling. To build a purse out of the package, fold over the triangle and pull the two bottom corners together. Put some water on the bottom corners to "glue" them together.

4. Keep going until all the wrappers and filling are gone.

5. A large, deep pot should be filled with oil until it reverses 375 degrees Fahrenheit, and it should be three inches deep.

6. Golden brown wontons may be achieved by frying 6-8 at a time for 3–5 minutes. Don't waste any of those wontons; simply drain them on paper towels and start over.

7. If you like sweet chili sauce, serve it on the side.

DUMPLINGS

Prep: 5 minutes

Cook:15 minutes

Ingredients

- 1 cup of all-purpose flour
- 2 tsp baking powder
- 1 tsp white sugar
- ½ tsp salt
- 1 tbsp margarine
- ½ cup of milk

Instructions

1. Put the flour, baking soda, sugar, and salt in a bowl and mix them together. To make a crumbly mixture, cut in butter. Add milk and continue mixing until a batter forms that can be scooped with a spoon. The batter has to rest for around 5 minutes.

2. Spoonfuls of batter can be tossed into a pot of simmering sauce. Maintain a low and steady simmer without disturbing the pot for 15 minutes. Serve.

PORK DUMPLINGS WITH PEANUT SAUCE

Preparation: 30 min

Cooking: 15 min

Ingredients

PEANUT SAUCE

- 3/4 cup of water
- 1/2 cup of crunchy peanut butter
- 1 tbsp honey
- 1 tbsp soy sauce; approximately
- 1 tsp sesame oil
- Salt and pepper

DUMPLINGS

- 1/2 lb (225g) lean ground pork
- 1 package of 20 grams dried shiitake mushrooms, rehydrated and chopped
- 1 green onion, chopped
- 1 tbsp fresh ginger, finely chopped
- 1 clove of garlic, finely chopped
- 1 tbsp soy sauce
- 1/2 tsp of sesame oil
- 34 squares won-ton wrappers or rounds sui mai wrappers
- 3 tbsp peanut oil or canola oil

Preparation

PEANUT SAUCE

Bring everything to a boil in a pot while whisking constantly. Reduce heat and simmer for 2–3 minutes, or until sauce thickens slightly. Put some salt and pepper on it. Putting aside.

DUMPLINGS

1. The pork, mushrooms, green onion, ginger, garlic, soy sauce, and sesame oil should all be mixed together in a bowl. Put some salt and pepper on it. Putting aside.

2. Place a stack of six wrappers on a flat surface. Place roughly 2 tsp, or 10 ml, of filling in the middle of every square with a spoon. Use a wet brush to dampen the wrappers, then fold them into a triangle or half moon. Avoid air bubbles by pressing the dough down around the filling before baking. Use the same procedure as the rest of the components.

3. Cook the dumplings for 2–3 minutes, or until they revery an al dente consistency, in a large saucepan of salted boiling water. Scrub and place on a baking sheet that has been greased.

4. Brown the dumplings on both sides in a large nonstick skillet using the mixed oils. Use peanut sauce as a condiment.

5. This is the point at which you can pause and freeze time. Reheat in the oven after thawing in the refrigerator.

DADDY'S SHRIMP TOAST

Prep: 25 minutes

Cook: 15 minutes

Ingredients

- 1 pound fresh shrimp, peeled, deveined, and finely minced
- ½ yellow onion, minced
- ½ cup of finely chopped water chestnuts
- ½ cup of finely chopped celery
- 1 green onion, finely chopped
- ½ cup of cooked crab meat
- 1 egg, beaten
- 1 ½ tbsp chopped fresh parsley

- 1 tsp sesame oil
- salt as need
- ground black pepper as needed
- 5 drops of soy sauce
- 1 tsp minced garlic
- 2 cups of oil for frying
- 8 thick slices of white bread
- ¼ cup of soy sauce
- 1 tbsp water
- 1 tsp sesame oil
- 3 tbsp chopped fresh parsley garlic powder as needed

Instructions

1. Add the shrimp, onion, water chestnuts, celery, and green onion to a mixing bowl. Add in the crab meat, egg, parsley, sesame oil, soy sauce, and garlic. Put in as much salt and pepper as you like.

2. Concoct the accompanying dipping sauce: Soy sauce, water, sesame oil, parsley, garlic powder, and sugar should be mixed in a small basin and placed away.

3. Over medium heat, heat 2 cups of oil in a heavy skillet, or enough to cover the bottom by 1/2 inch. Cover one side of every slice of bread with the shrimp filling.

4. Toast the toast in hot oil until golden brown, and the shrimp is pink, flipping once. If you want to ignore a soggy sandwich, don't let the filling stay on the bread for too long. Remove excess oil by draining on paper towels and waiting a minute. Cut on the diagonal for easy serving with or without sauce.

CHINESE DRY GARLIC SPARERIBS

Prep: 15 minutes

Cook: 45 minutes

Ingredients

- 3 pounds spareribs
- 1 1/2 cups of brown sugar, packed
- 1 1/2 cups of water
- 4 to 5 cloves of garlic
- 4 1/2 tbsp light soy sauce
- 1 1/2 tbsp dry mustard

Instructions

1. Assemble the necessary materials.
2. Start the boil on a big pot of water. Cook the ribs for 30 minutes at a low simmer with the lid on.
3. Brown sugar, water, garlic cloves, light soy sauce, and dry mustard should be mixed in a small basin while the spareribs boil.
4. Get the spareribs out of the stew and cut them in half through the meaty middle. (The pig broth can be saved for later use if desired.) Empty the cooking vessel.
5. Put all of the sauce ingredients in a saucepan and bring to a boil. After bringing the liquid back to a boil, reduce it to a simmer and baste the ribs frequently for 10 to 15 minutes.
6. Put the ribs out and put them on a plate. Simmer the sauce until it thickens, then pour it back over the ribs and serve.
7. Briefing on the Back Ribs
8. Since pork spare ribs are the most often eaten ribs, they should be easy to locate in the supermarket's meat case. Spareribs, which come from the lower part of the

rib cage (baby back ribs come from the upper part), are characterized by their flat bones and high-fat marbling. Every slab weighs around 3 pounds and contains roughly 11 bones. However, half of this weight is the bone, so if you think you're purchasing too much, divide the weight of the meat per person by the number of people for whom you're cooking. One slab of spareribs may usually be divided between two individuals. In addition, choose ribs with firm, pinkish-red flesh and no signs of discoloration.

9. Although they may be stored for up to six months in the freezer, fresh spareribs are best used within the first some days after purchase. You'll need at least 12 to 14 hours to defrost frozen ribs in the fridge, whether you've frozen them yourself or purchased them that way. Never attempt to cook cold ribs. Instead, give them 30 minutes to come to room temperature.

EGG DROP SOUP

Prep time: 5 minutes

Cook time: 10 minutes

Ingredients

- 4 cups of good-quality chicken or vegetable stock
- 2 tbsp cornstarch
- 2 tsp ground ginger
- 1 tsp garlic powder
- 1/8 tsp white pepper
- 3 large eggs
- 1 tsp toasted sesame oil
- fine sea salt and freshly-cracked black pepper, as need thinly-sliced green onions, for garnish

Instructions

1. Prepare the stock. In a saucepan, whisk together the stock (cold or room temperature), cornstarch, ginger, garlic powder, and white pepper. Simmer the stock over high heat while stirring periodically.

2. Scramble the eggs. While that is happening, in a separate small dish or measuring cup, mix the eggs and egg whites and whisk until mixed. (The measuring cup is more convenient for me while pouring.)

3. Put the egg ribbons in and mix. Once the broth is at a simmer, stir it with a whisk or two chopsticks in a whirlpool motion to aerate it. Then, while continuously swirling the soup, slowly pour the whisked eggs in a thin stream into the soup to make egg ribbons.

4. Season. Take the pan off the stove. The sesame oil should be stirred in until it is fully incorporated. Salt and white pepper as needed, and more sesame oil and/or salt if necessary. (The soup's saltiness may vary depending on the chicken stock you use, but typically I add an extra half to one tsp of fine sea salt.)

5. Serve. Garnish with heaps of green onions and a dash of black pepper, and serve right away.

HOT AND SOUR SOUP

Prep time: 5 minutes

Cook time: 15 minutes

Ingredients

- 8 cups of chicken broth
- 8 ounces of shiitake mushrooms
- 1 (8-ounce) can of bamboo shoots, drained (optional)
- 1/4 cup of rice vinegar, or more as needed
- 1/4 cup of low-sodium soy sauce
- 2 tsp ground ginger
- 1 tsp chili garlic sauce
- 1/4 cup of cornstarch
- 2 large eggs, whisked
- 8 ounces firm tofu cut into 1/2-inch cubes
- 4 green onions, thinly sliced
- 1 tsp toasted sesame oil
- Kosher salt and white pepper

Instructions

1. Reserve a quarter cup of the chicken or veggie broth.

2. Using a large stock pot, mix the remaining 7 3/4 cups of chicken or vegetable broth, the mushrooms, the bamboo shoots (if using), the rice wine vinegar, the soy sauce, the ginger, and the chili garlic sauce. The soup should be heated until it just begins to simmer over medium heat.

3. As the soup heats, make the thickening agent by whisking together the reserved 1/4 cup of stock and the cornstarch in a small basin. Once the soup is at a simmer, add the cornstarch mixture and cook, constantly stirring, for about a minute, until the soup thickens.

4. Egg ribbons may be made by continuing to swirl the soup in a circular motion while slowly pouring in the beaten eggs. Mix the tofu, half the green onions, and the sesame oil in a bowl. Add some salt and white pepper (or black pepper), as needed, to the soup. Soup may be made sourer by adding an extra tbsp or two of rice wine vinegar. Additional chili garlic sauce can be used for a hotter soup.

5. Prepare and serve right away, topping with the additional green onions.

WONTON SOUP

Prep: 20 minutes

Cook: 15 minutes

Ingredients

- 50 - 60 wonton wrappers

WONTON FILLING

- 7 oz lean pork mince
- 7 oz peeled prawns shrimp, roughly chopped
- 1 tbsp ginger, finely grated
- 2 green onions, finely chopped
- 1 tbsp light soy sauce
- 2 tbsp Chinese cooking wine
- 1/2 tsp salt
- 2 tbsp sesame oil, toasted

BROTH (FOR 2 SERVINGS)

- 3 cups of / 750 ml chicken broth
- 2 garlic cloves, smashed
- ⅓" / 1 cm piece of ginger, sliced
- 1½ tbsp light soy sauce
- 2 tsp sugar
- 1½ tbsp Chinese cooking wine
- ¼ - ½ tsp sesame oil

TO SERVE

- Shallots, scallions , finely chopped
- Bok choy quartered
- 1.5 oz dried egg noodles per person

Instructions

1. Gather the filling ingredients and set them aside. It should take around 20 mash strokes with a potato masher to get the consistency of smooth mashed potatoes. You don't want the prawns to turn into a paste, but you do want to leave some texture.

2. You may do it my way (for a more satisfying Wonton Soup) or the way they do it at Asian supermarkets (easier to pack for freezing).

3. Spread out the wontons on the counter. Put the filling on the wontons with 2 tbsp. Start with batches of 5 and increase to 15 or 20 as your confidence grows. Spray water down two borders and brush it on. With a firm fold and a little bit of air pressure, you can make a pretty good seal. One corner is wetted with a brush, and the other is brought in to form a seal.

4. Maintain freshness by storing wontons in an airtight container while you work.

5. For cooking, start by bringing a big pot of water to a boil. Cook wontons for 4 minutes or until they float. Get rid of using a slotted spoon and place it in serving dishes. Spoon the soup on top.

6. Pack uncooked food into sealed containers and freeze. Preparation time from frozen is about 6-8 minutes. It is crucial that if you have made this with defrosted frozen prawns, you must not freeze it.

7. Put the Broth ingredients into a pot and set it over high heat. If there are any white ends of scallions or shallots left over from the Wonton filling, add those.

8. Simmer, covered, for 5-10 minutes over medium heat to let the flavors blend. Sift through your groceries and separate the garlic cloves and ginger root.

9. To prepare veggies for serving, blanch them in the soup liquid.

10. Following the instructions on the noodle package to cook them. Place in a serving bowl with cooked wontons and blanched veggies.

11. Put in a soup ladle. Serve!

SINGAPORE NOODLES

Prep: 15 minutes

Cook: 10 minutes

Ingredients

SAUCE

- 2 tbsp soy sauce
- 2 tbsp Chinese cooking wine
- 2 1/2 tsp curry powder
- 1/2 tsp sugar
- 1/2 tsp white pepper

STIR FRY

- 100g / 3 oz dried rice vermicelli noodles
- 2 tbsp peanut oil, separated
- 8-10 medium raw shrimp prawns, shelled and deveined
- 2 eggs, beaten
- 1/2 medium onion, thinly sliced
- 4 garlic cloves, minced
- 1 tsp ginger, freshly grated
- 1/2 lb 250g Chinese barbecue pork
- 1 cup of red capsicum bell pepper
- 2 tsp thinly sliced hot green pepper

Instructions

1. Put the Sauce ingredients in a small bowl and stir to mix.
2. Soak rice vermicelli noodles in hot water for the time specified on the package. Retain the liquid, but put the draining water aside.
3. Over medium heat, bring 1 tbsp of oil to a wok or heavy-based frying pan. Toss in the shrimp or prawns and cook

for 2 1/2 to 3 minutes, or until they are pink but still firm. Do not use these; put them away.

4. Put in the egg and work it out into a thin omelet. After it has cooled, wrap it up with a spatula, take it out of the pan, and cut it into pieces (while still rolled up).

5. Place the wok back over medium heat and add the remaining tbsp of oil. Cook the garlic, ginger, and onion for 2 minutes or until the onion are somewhat softened.

6. Capsicum, add and heat for 1 minute.

7. Put in the noodle and sauce and stir it around a little. Then, stir in the egg, pork, shrimp/prawns, and chilies (if using). For about a minute and a half, or until the noodles are warm and the sauce is well distributed, toss them.

8. Don't wait around; serve right away.

BEEF CHOW FUN

PREP: 1 hour

COOK: 5 minutes

Ingredients

FOR THE BEEF & MARINADE:

- 8 oz. flank steak (225g, sliced into 1/8 thick pieces)
- 1/4 tsp baking soda (optional)
- 1 tsp cornstarch
- 1 tsp soy sauce
- 1 tsp vegetable oil

FOR THE REST OF THE DISH:

- 12 oz. fresh wide rice noodles
- 3 tbsp vegetable oil
- 4 scallions
- 3 thin slices of ginger
- 2 tbsp Shaoxing wine
- 1/2 tsp sesame oil
- 2 tsp dark soy sauce
- 2 tbsp regular soy sauce
- 1/8 tsp sugar
- salt and white pepper (as needed)
- 4 to 6 ounces of fresh mung bean sprouts

Instructions

1. Marinate the beef for about an hour using the marinade ingredients.

2. Fresh rice noodles can be purchased in either huge sheets or pre- portioned servings. Cut the rice noodles into 1-inch lengths if you have the sheets available. Take a wok of

water to a boil, and then add the noodles if they are extremely stiff and stuck together. To loosen them, boil water over them for 30 seconds. Drain well before placing it in an ice bath.

3. You should use 1 and a half tsp of oil to coat the wok and cook it over high heat until it is smoking. Stir in the steak and brown it in the pan. If your wok is hot enough, you won't have to worry about the meat sticking. Putting aside. The work will need an additional 1 1/2 tsp of vegetable oil. After around 15 seconds, add the ginger and let it saturate the oil with its robust flavor. Throw in some scallions.

4. Arrange the noodles in a single layer in the wok and stir-fry for a maximum of 15 seconds at high heat. In a circular motion around the edge of the wok, pour in the Shaoxing wine.

5. Then, throw in some seared meat, sesame oil, and soy sauce with a dash of sugar. When creating a stir-fry, it's important to have the bottom of the wok scraped with a metal spatula. To uniformly cover the noodles with the sauce, lift them up and do a little dance.

6. Salt and white pepper as needed (taste the noodles before adding salt). Throw in some bean sprouts and cook them in a stir-fry until they're soft. Serve!

PORK CHOW MEIN

Prep: 15 min

Marinating

Cook: 15 min

Ingredients

- 1 pound boneless pork loin
- 2 garlic cloves, minced
- 4 tbsp soy sauce, divided
- 2 tbsp cornstarch
- 1/2 to 1 tsp ground ginger
- 1 cup of chicken broth
- 1 tbsp canola oil
- 1 cup of thinly sliced carrots
- 1 cup of thinly sliced celery
- 1 cup of chopped onion
- 1 cup of coarsely chopped cabbage
- 1 cup of coarsely chopped fresh spinach
- Hot cooked rice, optional

Directions

1. Put the pork in a basin and slice it into four-by-quarter-inch slices. Two tsp of soy sauce and garlic should be added. Make sure to cover and chill for at least two hours.

2. While that's happening, whisk together some cornstarch, ginger, broth, and the rest of the soy sauce. Stir-fry the pork in a large pan or wok with some oil heated over high heat until the meat is no longer pink.

3. Taking out and keeping warm. Stir-fry the carrots and celery for three to four minutes. Stir-fry for 2–3 minutes after adding the onion, cabbage, and spinach. Mix the

broth and seasonings in a bowl, then add to the pork in the skillet and stir. Achieve a boil, then continue cooking and stirring for another 3–4 minutes, or until the mixture has thickened. The rice can be served immediately if desired.

SHRIMP LO MEIN RECIPE

Prep Time: 10 minutes

Cook time: 10 minutes

Ingredients

- 16 ounces of Chinese egg noodles
- 3 tbsp Coconut oil
- 1 cup of sliced Chinese sausage
- ½ pound shrimp peeled and deveined, tail removed
- ¼ tsp ground black pepper
- ¼ tsp ground white pepper
- ¼ cup of chopped green onion
- 2 cloves garlic minced
- 1 tsp fresh grated ginger
- 1 red bell pepper diced
- 3 baby bok choy chopped into bite-size pieces
- 1 cup of snow peas
- For the Sauce
- 2 tbsp. soy sauce
- 1 ½ tbsp. oyster sauce
- 1 tbsp. Shaoxing wine
- ½ tbsp. honey
- ½ tsp. sesame oil

Instructions

1. Dry noodles should be prepared according to package directions, drained, and kept aside.
2. Whisk together the sauce ingredients and leave aside.
3. Smoke the coconut oil in a heavy skillet or wok over high heat.

4. Toss shrimp with black and white pepper after drying them with paper towels. Stir-fry for 1-2 minutes, or until they become pink, then remove from pan with a slotted spatula and put aside. If you want to avoid having the shrimp steam instead of stir-fry, it's better to cook them in batches.

5. Stir fry the Chinese sausage for about 2 minutes, or until it begins to brown on the outside. Take out and set aside.

6. Ginger and garlic should be added, and they should sizzle for around 30 seconds. Pepper, peas, scallions, and bok choy should be added (or any other vegetable you decide to use). Stir-fry for 2 minutes, then take out using a slotted spoon.

7. Toss in the noodles and bring the heat back up to high for 3 to 4 minutes or until they begin to develop light charred areas.

8. The veggies, shrimp, sausage, and sauce should all be placed in the pan. Cook for a further minute or two, occasionally stirring with tongs, until the sauce has thickened and covered the noodles. Take it off the heat and serve.

FRIED RICE

Prep time: 5 minutes

Cook time: 10 minutes

Ingredients

- 3 tbsp butter, divided
- 2 large eggs, whisked
- 2 medium carrots, peeled and diced
- 1 small white onion, diced
- 1/2 cup of frozen peas
- 3 cloves garlic, minced salt and black pepper
- 4 cups of cooked and chilled rice
- 3 green onions, thinly sliced
- 4 tbsp soy sauce
- 2 tsp oyster sauce (optional)
- 1/2 tsp toasted sesame oil

Instructions

1. In a large sauté pan, melt half a tbsp of butter over medium heat. Cook the egg, stirring periodically until it is scrambled. Put the egg out and set it aside.

2. To the already melted butter in the pan, add another tbsp. Toss in some carrots, onions, peas, and garlic, then season with salt and pepper as needed. The onion and carrots should be sautéed for about 5 minutes or until they are tender. Put the stove on high and add the remaining 1 1/2 tsp of butter, constantly stirring, until it melts. Soy sauce and oyster sauce (if used) should be added right away, followed by the rice. To saute the rice, keep the pan on medium heat for a further 3 minutes, stirring periodically. (I prefer to wait a few minutes in between stirrings so the bottom of the rice may get crispy.) Then, crack in the eggs and mix everything together. Turn off the stove and

mix in the sesame oil. If more soy sauce is desired, taste and add.

3. Either consume immediately away or put in the refrigerator in an airtight container for up to three days.

YOUNG CHOW FRIED RICE

Prep:30 minutes

Cook:10 minutes

Ingredients

- 5 cups of cooked rice
- 3 tbsp oil
- 2 large eggs (beaten)
- 4 ounces of fresh shrimp
- 1 medium onion (finely diced)
- 1/2 cup of Virginia ham, cut into cubes
- 1/2 cup of Chinese Roast Pork
- 3/4 cup of frozen peas (thawed)
- 1 1/2 tsp salt
- ¼ tsp sugar
- 1 tsp Shaoxing wine (optional)
- 2 scallions (finely chopped)
- 2 cups of iceberg lettuce
- 1/8 tsp freshly ground white pepper

Instructions

1. Rice should be prepared in accordance with the package's instructions. Use a little less water than called for in any fried rice recipe if you don't want a mushy, sticky mess that won't stir-fry well. Keep the lid off while the rice cools. When the rice has finished cooking, and the steam has subsided, fluff it with a fork to separate the grains. If there are any remaining clumps, don't fret; they may be broken up in the wok.

2. Refrigerating the rice overnight will cause it to clump, but you can simply separate the grains by hand. If your

hands become too sticky, just rinse them with cold water at regular intervals.

3. Put 1 tbsp of oil into a hot pan and then add the beaten eggs. Gently scramble and fold them, being careful not to burn the eggs. The eggs should be returned to the original egg dish and left aside. The shrimp should be blanched in water that has been brought to a boil and then drained. Putting aside.

4. Put the wok over high heat right away. Include the chopped onion and 2 tbsp of oil. Make sure the onions are cooked through before serving. After that, throw in some diced ham and pork and give everything a quick 30-second stir-fry. Stir-fry the rice for 2 minutes, making sure it heats up evenly. Any remaining rice clumps can be broken up and spread out with a wok spatula. To heat the rice, add the shrimp and peas and continue to stir-fry for 2 minutes.

5. Then, season the rice with salt and sugar. If used, Shaoxing should be drizzled around the edge of the wok to create a good sizzle and to cook off some of the wine's alcohol. Mix all of the ingredients and stir to make sure the seasonings are well distributed.

6. Be cautious not to overdo it with the water or chicken stock; too much of either will make the rice mushy and oily. If the rice appears dry, feel free to add extra. If you have rice that has clumped together, you may separate the grains by adding liquid straight to the clumps.

7. Just to recap: 1. Summertime meals taste better when eaten al fresco. (2) Outside food is welcome; it adds to the evening's ambiance. Enjoy!

8. Then, stir in the chopped lettuce, scallions, and white pepper with the scrambled eggs. Mix everything together and stir-fry until the lettuce is wilted.

TWICE-COOKED PORK

Prep:10 minutes

Cook:35 minutes

Ingredients

- 1 pound pork belly
- 2 slices ginger
- 2 tbsp oil (divided)
- 1 1/2 tbsp spicy broad bean paste
- 2 cloves garlic (sliced)
- 2 long hot green peppers
- 1 medium leek
- 1 tbsp Shaoxing wine
- 1 tsp soy sauce
- 1/4 tsp sugar

Instructions

1. Put two quarts of water over high heat in a standard-sized saucepan. Bring the water back to a boil and add the entire pork belly and ginger. Once boiling, reduce the heat to a simmer and cook for 30 minutes, or until meat is tender. After approximately a minutes in the boiling water, drain the pork and rinse it under cold running water. Place aside.

2. Make the rest of the sauce while the pork is cooling. The pork belly should be thinly sliced (approximately 1/8 inch thick) and cooked as soon as possible (not ahead of time, because the meat would dry up).

3. The wok should be heated until it begins to smoke over high heat. To create a mild caramelization on the pork, sear it for around 90 seconds in 1 tbsp of oil. To remove the pork, reduce the heat to medium. In the wok, pour in an extra tbsp of oil.

4. Fry the spicy broad bean paste for 30 seconds in the oil to bring out the flavor and color, then add it to the wok. Red is the correct hue, and caution should be exercised around the fire.

5. Now, stir in the garlic and cook for 30 second. Put the pork, peppers, and leeks into a pan and crank up the heat. Cook in a wok for one minute. Shaoxing wine, soy sauce, and sugar should be added. Mix it everything together in a pot. It's done when the leeks have wilted, and the peppers are tender but still have some crunch.

MOO SHU PORK

Prep: 10 minutes

Cook: 10 minutes

Ingredients

- Marinade
- ½ cup of orange juice
- ½ cup of hoisin sauce
- 2 tbsp soy sauce
- 2 tsp sesame oil
- 4 cloves garlic minced
- 2 tsp cornstarch
- Moo Shu Pork
- 1 pound pork chops boneless, sliced thinly, or pork tenderloin
- 3 tbsp peanut oil
- 1 cup of red cabbage shredded
- 8-ounce shiitake mushrooms sliced
- 3 green onions chopped into
- 1" pieces, cut on the diagonal
- ½ cup of radishes sliced

Instructions

1. To marinate the pork, mix all the marinade ingredients together in a plastic bag. Keep aside a half cup of the marinade. Put the pork in a plastic bag and toss it around so that the marinade covers every piece of meat. Put aside for 5 minutes.

2. To prepare, heat the peanut oil in a big pan set over high heat. Place the meat that has been marinating in the bag into the skillet. Lightly brown the pork in a skillet over medium heat, breaking it up with tongs every 2

to 3 minutes. Cook the veggies for 3-4 minute, or until they revery a fork-tender consistency. Cook for one more minute, often stirring, to thicken the sauce, and then stir in the half cup of sauce set aside earlier.

3. To serve, spoon into Chinese pancakes or tortillas and top with extra hoisin sauce. Green onions and radishes work well as garnishes.

SHANGHAI-STYLE PORK CHOPS

Prep: 45 minutes

Cook: 15 minutes

Ingredients

- 1 pound pork tenderloin
- 4 eggs divided
- ½ tsp white pepper
- 2 tbsp light soy sauce
- 1 tbsp Shaoxing wine
- 1½ tbsp oyster sauce
- 1 tsp cornstarch
- Vegetable oil for deep frying
- ½ cup of all-purpose flour
- 1½ cups of panko breadcrumbs

FOR THE DIPPING SAUCE:

- 1½ tbsp light soy sauce
- 1 tbsp Chinese black vinegar
- ½ tsp sugar
- 1 tsp Worcestershire sauce
- 3 tbsp water
- Chili oil, as need

Instructions

1. The pork tenderloin should be washed and dried with a paper towel or kitchen towel. At a 30-degree angle, cut the pork into pieces about 2 inches thick. Then, used either a rolling pin or the blade of a knife, pound the meat until it is approximately 1/2 inch thick. If you want to avoid damaging the material, avoid pounding it too thin.

2. Mix 2 beaten eggs, 1/2 tsp white pepper powder, 1 tbsp Shaoxing wine, 2 tsp light soy sauce, 112 tbsp oyster sauce, and 1 tsp cornstarch for the marinade. Toss all the ingredient together and let them marinate for 30 minutes.

3. Next, whip up some sauce to dip the food in. Prepare a marinade using 1 1/2 tsp of light soy sauce, 1 tbsp of black vinegar, 1/2 tsp of sugar, 1 tsp of Worcestershire sauce, 3 tbsp of water, and chile oil as needed. Mix and set aside.

4. Put the vegetable oil into a frying pan so that it covers the bottom by about an inch. Warm it up over low heat first. While that is going on, beat 2 eggs in a big bowl. Half a cup of all-purpose flour should be placed in one bowl, while one and a half cups of panko should be placed in another.

5. Just dust the pork chop with flour and rapidly dip it in the beaten egg to coat. When you're ready, coat it with panko breadcrumbs. The panko flakes should be pressed firmly into the pork chop to create a substantial coating. You'll need to do this again and again until all of the pork is covered.

6. Fry the pork chops in batches for about a minute and a half on every side, then remove to paper towels to drain. When the crust becomes golden brown, they are done. The pork chops will taste much better if they are not overcooked. The majority of folks overcook their pork. They ought to be juicy! Move the pork to a wire rack or dish lined with paper towels between batches.

7. For serving, slice the pork chop into thick pieces and serve with the homemade dipping sauce.

CHINESE SPARE RIBS

Prep: 5 minutes

Cook: 40 minutes

Ingredients

- 3 tbsp hoisin sauce
- 1 tbsp ketchup
- 1 tbsp honey
- 1 tbsp soy sauce
- 1 tbsp sake
- 1 tsp rice vinegar
- 1 tsp lemon juice
- 1 tsp grated fresh ginger
- ½ tsp grated fresh garlic
- ¼ tsp Chinese five-spice powder
- 1 pound of pork spareribs

Instructions

1. Blend together in a glass bowl the following: hoisin sauce, ketchup, honey, soy sauce, sake, rice vinegar, lemon juice, ginger, garlic, and five-spice powder. Coat the ribs by placing them in the dish and turning them over. Place in a covered container and marinate for at least 2 hours and up to a whole night in the fridge.

2. Setingt the temperature to 325 degree Fahrenheit. Make sure the water in the broiler tray reverses to the very bottom. A grate or rack may be set up on top of the tray, and the ribs can be placed there.

3. Turn and baste with marinade every 10 minute while roasting for 40 minutes in the oven's middle rack. In last 10 minutes, let the marinade reduce to a glaze. You may broil it to a crisp finish if you like. Throw away any leftover marinade.

SWEET AND SOUR PORK RECIPE

Prep Time30 minutes Cook Time30 minutes

Ingredients

- 1 lb pork sliced
- 1 piece of red bell pepper
- 1 piece of green bell pepper
- 3 tbsp soy sauce
- 1 piece of red onion wedged
- 1 piece carrot sliced
- 1/2 cup of all-purpose flour
- 3 tbsp cornstarch
- Sweet and Sour Sauce
- 1 1/4 cup of water
- 3 1/2 tbsp vinegar
- 5 tbsp tomato ketchup
- 4 tbsp white sugar
- Salt and pepper as needed

Instructions

1. In a bowl, lay out the pork loin. Soy sauce, please (you may also add salt if desired). Please allow 10 minutes for the marinating process.
2. Add the oil to the pan and turn on the stove.
3. To make sure the flour and cornstarch are uniformly distributed, mix them in a bowl and stir until everything is mixed.
4. First, you'll want to coat the pork that has been marinating in beaten egg, and then in the flour and cornstarch.

5. Coat the pork with cornstarch and flour, then deep-fried it for 10 minutes, or until it reverses a medium brown color. Reserved for later use.

6. Put the sweet and sour sauce ingredients into a separate skillet and heat them up. Bring to a boil.

7. Toss in some carrots. The recommended cooking time is 3 minutes.

8. Chop and add onions and peppers (green and red). Set timer for 4 minutes (add extra water as needed).

9. Mix in the deep-fried pork loin. The recommended cooking time is 2 minutes. Add salt and pepper as needed.

10. Place on a heated serving plate and serve immediately. Let's all have fun together.

CHINESE PORK STIR FRY WITH SNOW PEAS

Prep Time 15 minutes Cook Time 10 minutes

Ingredients

- 4 pork chops, thinly sliced
- 1 pound of snow peas
- 1 1/2 cups of water (divided)
- 1/4 cup of soy sauce
- 3 tbsp sugar
- 1/4 tsp ground ginger
- 2 tbsp corn starch
- 2 tbsp vegetable oil for frying

Instructions

1. Set a large frying pan over moderate heat. Fifteen milliliters of vegetable oil, please.

2. Stir fry the pork for about five minutes, or until it is nearly done cooking, after adding it to the heated oil.

3. Put in 1 1/4 cups of water, 1/4 cup of soy sauce, and 3 tsp of sugar.

4. Put in the ground ginger and snow peas. Cook in a stir-fry until the pea pods are crisp-tender (about five minutes).

5. Mix the corn starch and water (2 tbsp + 1/4 cup of). Add to the meat and peas and constantly stir until the sauce thickens.

6. Accompany rice or noodles for a traditional Chinese meal.

GARLIC BUTTER STEAK BITES

Prep: 5 minutes

Cook: 10 minutes

Ingredients

- 1 tbsp olive oil
- 1 ½ lb sirloin steak cut into bite-size piece
- ½ tsp salt or as need
- ½ tsp pepper or as need
- 2 tbsp butter unsalted
- 4 cloves garlic minced
- ¼ tsp red pepper flakes
- 1tbsp parsley fresh, chopped

Instructions

1. Prepare the olive oil by placing it in a big pan and heating it over high heat. Before adding the steak, test the temperature of the olive oil. Sprinkle a lot of salt and pepper over them.

2. Do not stir the steak for at least two minutes after it has been placed in the oven. Be careful to give them a nice sear. To get a golden brown color, cook for an additional 2 minutes. You may need to do this in two separate batches if your skillet is too small.

3. After removing the steak bits to a platter, melt the butter in the same pan. After the butter melts, reduce the heat to medium and add the garlic and red pepper flakes. Cook the garlic for about 30 second until it releases its pungent scent and turns golden brown.

4. Toss the steak bites with the garlic butter. Served with a sprinkle of chopped parsley on top.

SZECHUAN BEEF

Prep: 10 minutes

Cook: 10 minutes

Ingredients

- 1 pound sirloin steak, cut into bite-size strips
- 1 tbsp soy sauce
- 2 tsp cornstarch
- ¼ tsp crushed red pepper
- 1 clove of garlic, minced
- 2 tbsp vegetable oil
- 3 cups of fresh broccoli florets
- 2 small onions, cut into wedges
- 1 (8 ounces) can of water chestnuts, drained
- ¼ cup of chicken broth
- ½ cup of peanuts

Instructions

1. Mix the meat with the soy sauce, cornstarch, crushed red pepper, and garlic in a bowl made of a non-corrosive material. Put in the fridge for 20 minutes, covered.

2. Oil should be heated in a wok or a big pan set over high heat. Beef should be cooked for 5 minutes in a stir fry until it is no longer pink. Add in the water chestnuts, onions, and broccoli and sauté for another 2 minutes. Toss in some broth and get it boiling. Cook for a further minute while stirring in the peanuts.

BEEF CHOP SUEY (BEEF STIR FRY)

Prep Time: 10 minutes

Cook time: 20 minutes

Ingredients

- 2 tbsp butter
- 1 onion - chopped
- 2 stalks of celery - finely chopped
- 2 tsp ginger - minced
- 2 cloves garlic - minced
- 2 pounds hamburger
- 2 tbsp molasses
- ¼ cup of soy sauce
- 2 tbsp cornstarch
- 1 cup of hot water
- 1 small can of water chestnuts - drained
- 1 large can of bean sprouts - drained
- 4 cups of rice - cooked

Instructions

1. In a large pan over medium heat, cook the onion and celery in the butter for about 5 minutes. Cook for a another minute or so after adding the ginger and garlic.

2. Turn up the heat to medium-high and throw in some ground meat. Brown it to your liking.

3. Add the soy sauce and molasses and mix well. Cornstarch and water should be mixed together, then added to the steak and cooked until the sauce thickens, stirring often.

4. Add the water chestnuts and bean sprouts and simmer for two more minutes, stirring occasionally.

5. Serve over rice with a spoonful.

STIR-FRIED BEEF WITH OYSTER SAUCE

Prep:10 minutes

Cook:10 minutes

Ingredients

- 450g lean beef steak
- 1 tbsp light soy sauce
- 2 tsp sesame oil
- 1 tbsp Shaoxing rice wine
- 2 tsp cornflour
- 3 tbsp groundnut oil
- 1 red pepper, cut
- 1 green pepper, cut
- 3 tbsp oyster sauce
- 2 spring onions, finely shredded, to garnish

Method

1. Reduce the beef to 5mm thick by cutting it into 5cm long strips against the grain. Drop them into a basin. Whisk in the cornstarch, rice wine (or Sherry), sesame oil, and soy sauce. Let sit for 20 minute to absorb the flavors.

2. Prepare the groundnut oil by heating a wok until extremely hot. Add the beef slice and stir-fry for 5 minutes, or until gently browned, after the oil is hot enough to smoke. Remove the meat from the pan and let it cool while being drained in a strainer over water. Throw away the used oil.

3. After cleaning, place the wok back over high heat. Add the peppers and simmer for another 3–4 minutes, or until they have softened. Simmer the mixture after adding the oyster sauce. Drain the beef pieces, then return them to the pan and stir them in the oyster sauce. Sprinkle the spring onion on top of the mixture and serve immediately.

GINGER BEEF

Prep: 15 minutes

Cook: 15 minutes

Ingredients

- 1 pound flank steak cut into 1/4" thin strips
- 2-3 cups of vegetable oil for frying

Batter

- 1 cup of cornstarch
- ¼ cup of all-purpose flour
- 1 tsp white pepper
- ¾ cup of water
- 1 egg

Sauce

- ⅓ cup of soy sauce low sodium
- ¼ cup of water
- 2 tbsp dark soy sauce
- 2 tbsp rice vinegar
- ⅓ cup of brown sugar packed
- 1 tsp chili flakes
- Stir fry
- 1 tbsp sesame oil
- 5 cloves garlic minced
- 1 tbsp fresh ginger, minced
- 1 tbsp sesame seeds
- 2 green onions thinly sliced

Instructions

1. To prepare the beef for battering, slice the flank steak against the grain into thin strips measuring 1/4 inch thick. To facilitate slicing, freezing the meat for 10-20 minutes may be useful. Mix the flour, cornstarch, and white pepper in a large bowl and whisk until smooth. Whisk in the water and egg until the batter is completely smooth. The beef strips should be tossed in the batter to get coated.

2. To fry the beef, fill a saucepan with vegetable oil until it is about two to three inches high. Bring the oil up to a temperature of 350 degrees Fahrenheit. Toss in the beef strips in batches and toss and shred them with a fork as they cook. Golden brown in 3 to 4 minutes of frying. With a slotted spoon, take out the beef strips and set them on a platter covered with paper towels to absorb any excess oil.

3. To prepare the sauce, heat the ingredients by whisking them together in a bowl. The sesame oil should be heated in a large pan over medium heat. Throw in some garlic and ginger, and let them simmer for a minute or until they start to release their aroma. Take the sauce in the pan and cook it over medium heat, occasionally stirring, for about two minutes, or until it has thickened somewhat.

4. After the beef strips have been cooked, add them to the skillet and toss them in the sauce so that they are well covered. Continue cooking for a further minute or two, or until the meat is well coated with sauce. Green onion and sesame seeds provide a great finishing touch.

PEPPER STEAK STIR FRY

Prep Time10 minutes Cook Time20 minutes

Ingredients

- 1 tbsp vegetable oil divided use
- 1 red bell pepper cored
- 1 green bell pepper cored, seeded
- 1 1/4 pounds flank steak thinly sliced
- 2 tsp minced garlic
- 1 tsp minced ginger
- salt and pepper as needed
- 1/4 cup of soy sauce
- 1 1/2 tbsp sugar
- 1 1/2 tbsp cornstarch

Instructions

1. In a skillet, heat 1 tsp of the vegetable oil over medium heat.

2. Cook the peppers for 3–4 minutes, or until they revery the desired tenderness. Put the peppers on a dish and take them out of the pan.

3. Put the rest of the oil in the skillet. Taste the steak and season with salt and pepper as desired.

4. Amp up the temperature to high. Put the steak in the pan and brown it on all sides, which should take around 5 to 6 minutes.

5. Cook the garlic and ginger for 30 second after adding them.

6. Peppers should be re-added to the meat in the pan.

7. Mix the soy sauce, sugar, 1/4 cup of water, and cornstarch together in a small bowl.

8. Toss the sauce into the steak mixture and lower the heat to a simmer. Leave to simmer for two to three minutes, or until sauce has thickened somewhat, then serve.

EASY BEEF AND BROCCOLI

Prep time: 10 minutes

Cook time: 10 minutes

Ingredients

- 3 Tbsp cornstarch divided
- 1 lb flank steak, cut
- 1/2 cup of low sodium soy sauce
- 3 Tbsp packed light brown sugar
- 1 Tbsp minced garlic
- 2 tsp grated fresh ginger
- 2 Tbsp vegetable oil, divided
- 4 cups of small broccoli florets
- 1/2 cup of sliced white onions

Instructions

1. Blend 2 tbsp. Of cornstarch and 3 tbsp. of water in a big bowl. Throw the meat into the mixing basin and stir it around.

2. Mix the remaining 1 tbsp of cornstarch, the soy sauce, brown sugar, garlic, and ginger in a separate small dish and whisk until smooth. Don't use the sauce yet.

3. Preheat a large, nonstick sauté pan over medium heat. Once the oil is heated, add the steak and continue cooking it while stirring regularly until it is almost done. The meat may be removed from the pan using a slotted spoon and left aside.

4. When the pan is heated, add the remaining tbsp of vegetable oil and then the broccoli florets and the sliced onions. Cook for approximately 4 minutes, turning periodically until the broccoli is cooked.

5. Bring the meat back into the pan and top it with the sauce you made. To make a thicker sauce, bring the ingredients

to a boil and simmer, constantly stirring, for 1 minute.
Accompany with noodles or rice.

65

KUNG PAO BEEF

Prep Time: 10 minutes

Cook time: 20 minutes

Ingredients

For the stir fry

- 2 tbsp vegetable oil divided use
- 1 1/4 pounds flank steak thinly sliced
- 1 1/2 tbsp cornstarch
- 1 red bell pepper
- 1 green bell pepper
- 1/2 cup of onion
- 1 1/2 tsp garlic minced
- 4-6 dried red chilies seeded and cut in half
- 1/2 cup of roasted unsalted peanuts
- salt and pepper as needed

For the sauce

- 3 tbsp low sodium soy sauce
- 1 1/2 tbsp hoisin sauce
- 1 tbsp toasted sesame oil
- 1 tbsp granulated sugar
- 1 tbsp cornstarch
- 1/4 cup of water

Instructions

For the stir fry

1. Put the 1 1/2 tablespoons of vegetable oil in a pan and heat it over high heat until it is extremely hot. Mix the

steak, cornstarch, and seasonings as needed in a medium bowl. Blend ingredients by giving them a little toss.

2. Arrange the meat in the pan in a single layer. Fry every side for about three minutes to get a golden color. This process may need you to work in bunches.

3. Take the meat out of the skillet. Keep warm by wrapping yourself in foil.

4. Replace some of the olive oil that was used up with vegetable oil. Throw in some onion and red and green peppers. Vegetables should be cooked for four to five minutes or until they are tender.

5. Sauté the garlic for 30 seconds after adding it to the pan. Put the steak back in the skillet. Mix in the peanuts and the chiles.

For the sauce

1. Prepare the sauce while the meat and veggies are cooking. Put everything in a little bowl and mix it up with a whisk.

2. Bring the beef mixture to a boil, then add the sauce and let it cook 1 minute. Rapid service is required.

SESAME BEEF

Prep: 5 minutes

Cook: 10 minutes

Ingredients

- 1 pound round steak
- 4 tbsp soy sauce
- 4 tbsp white sugar
- 4 tbsp vegetable oil
- 2 cloves garlic, minced
- 2 green onions, chopped
- 2 tbsp sesame seeds

Instructions

1. Mix the sugar, oil, garlic, and onions with the soy sauce in a large bowl. Ignore it for the time being.

2. Don't forget to add your steak slices to the bowl. Place in the fridge for at least 30 minute, preferably overnight.

3. Approximately 5 minutes of cooking time should be plenty in a wok or frying pan to get a golden brown color. For an extra 2 minute of cooking time, add the sesame seeds.

CLASSIC ORANGE BEEF

Active: 35 minutes

Total: 1 hr 20 minutes

Ingredients

- 1/2 pound flank steak thinly sliced
- 1 tsp baking soda
- 1 large orange, zest removed in strips
- 3 tbsp soy sauce
- 3 tbsp white vinegar
- 2 tbsp sake
- 2 tbsp sugar
- 2 tsp plus 1/2 cup of cornstarch
- 1 large egg white
- 2 cups of peanut oil for frying
- 1 tsp kosher salt
- 3 scallions, thinly sliced
- 1 tsp Asian chili-garlic paste
- 1 tsp toasted sesame oil

Instructions

1. The steak should be dusted with baking soda and tossed in a shallow basin to coat. Place it in the fridge and let it chill for 30 minutes.

2. Whisk together the soy sauce, vinegar, sake, sugar, and 2 tsp of cornstarch in a glass measuring cup.

3. Throw the meat into the egg white and toss to coat. Then, sprinkle the meat with the remaining 1/2 cup of cornstarch and toss it once more to coat it. Wait 10 minutes before consuming. During this time, heat the peanut oil to 375 degrees Fahrenheit in a wok over moderately high heat.

4. Prepare the meat by frying it in three separate batches in
    the heated oil until it is crisp and lightly browned, about
    4 minutes every batch. Every time you fry anything, place
    it on a baking sheet lined with paper towels and sprinkle
    with a third of a tsp of kosher salt.

5. Remove all of the oil from the pan except for 1 tbsp. Once
    the oil is hot, add the orange zest strips and stir-fry for
    approximately a minute or until the zest is aromatic and
    lightly browned. Continue cooking for one more minute
    after adding the scallions and chile paste. Orange juice
    and soy sauce should be whisked together, then added to
    the pot and brought to a boil; the sauce should be cooked
    for about 1 minute or until it has thickened. Take the meat
    back in the pan and mix it with the sauce to coat. Mix the
    sesame oil with the dish and serve.

EMPRESS CHICKEN

Ready in: 45minutes

Ingredients

- 1 1/2 cups of chicken broth
- 3/4 cup of sugar
- 1/4 - 1/2 cup of cornstarch
- 1/2 cup of soy sauce
- 1/2 cup of white vinegar
- 3 -4 garlic cloves, minced
- 1 1/2 tsp fresh ginger, chopped
- 3 lbs boneless skinless chicken breasts, cubed
- 1/4 cup of dark soy sauce (tamari)
- 1 large egg, beaten
- 1/2 cup of cornstarch
- 2 cups of green onions, minced (one bunch)
- 8 small hot peppers, diced (I used jalapenos)

Directions

1. Shake the first seven ingredients together in a container until well- mixed. Keep refrigerated until ready to use.
2. Mix the chicken with 1/4 cup of dark soy sauce. Add egg and mix.
3. Chicken, cornstarch, and a mixing bowl.
4. Fry in a pot of heated oil, occasionally turning, until golden brown.
5. Get rid of the water using paper towels.
6. Warm a some tbsp of oil in a wok over high heat.
7. Stir-fry the onion and pepper for 30 seconds.
8. Mix in the sauce ingredients (shake again first).

9. Prepare until thick. If the mixture becomes too thick, simply dilute it with water.

10. Add the chicken and continue cooking until everything is hot and bubbling.

11. Pour over steaming rice.

MOO GOO GAI PAN

Prep Time: 30 minutes

Cook Time: 15 minutes

Ingredients

- 1 lb of boneless skinless chicken breasts
- 1 large egg white
- 2 tbsp + 1 tsp of cornstarch divided use
- 1 tbsp vegetable oil divided use
- 2 tsp minced garlic
- 1 tsp minced ginger
- 2 cups of sliced mushrooms
- 1 cup of snow peas
- 1/2 cup of thinly sliced carrots
- 1 8-oz of sliced water chestnuts drained
- 1 8-oz of sliced bamboo shoots drained
- 3/4 cup of chicken stock
- 1 1/2 tsp sugar
- 1 tbsp soy sauce
- 1 1/2 tsp sesame oil
- salt and pepper as needed

Instructions

1. Mix the egg white and the tbsp of cornstarch in a medium bowl and whisk until smooth. Toss in the chicken strips and cover everything evenly. After chilling for 30 minutes, drain off the liquid and throw it away.

2. One tsp of oil should be heated over medium heat in a big pot. Carrots and 1 tbsp water should be added and cooked for 2-3 minutes while being stirred often.

3. Toss in the fungi, and cook for three to four minutes until they're browned and soft.

4. Once the onions are translucent, add the snow peas and simmer for a further minute or two. Stir in the water chestnuts and bamboo stalks. Add salt and pepper as needed before serving the veggies.

5. Take the veggie out of the skillet and set them on a platter. You may keep the food warm by wrapping the plate with foil.

6. Paper towel the pan clean. Two more tbsp of oil should be heated in a skillet.

7. Take the chicken in the pan and season it with salt and pepper as needed. When the chicken is fully cooked, which should take around 3-4 minutes, remove it from the heat and stir. Cook for another 30 second after adding the garlic and ginger.

8. Chicken stock, sugar, and soy sauce, sesame oil are mixed in a small bowl and whisked together. Mix cornstarch and water by whisking in 1 tbsp.

9. Place the veggie back in the pan and cook them for a minute or so until they're hot all the way through. Put the sauce in and set the stove to high. To thicken the sauce, bring it to a boil and keep it there for about a minute, stirring regularly.

10. It's best served right away, preferably over rice.

LEMON CHICKEN

Prep time: 5 min

Cook time: 30 min

Ingredients

- 3 to 4 pounds of chicken parts
- 4 tsp lemon zest
- 1/3 cup of lemon juice
- 2 cloves garlic, crushed

Method

- 2 tbsp fresh chopped thyme
- 2 tsp fresh chopped rosemary
- 1 tsp kosher salt
- 1 tsp black pepper
- 2 tbsp butter, melted
- Lemon slices for garnish

1. Put all the ingredients for the dressing (lemon juice, lemon zest, garlic, thyme, rosemary, salt, and pepper) into a large nonreactive bowl and mix them together.

2. One or two shallow cuts, about half an inch deep, made with the point of a sharp knife, should be made into the underside (skinless) of every piece of chicken.

3. Toss the chicken in the marinade and flip to coat every piece. Marinate for at least an hour, preferably up to two, in the fridge.

4. Baked chicken with a butter coating:

5. Set the temperature in the oven up to 425 degrees. Take chicken out of the marinade and put in a single layer in a large baking dish, skin side up. Be sure to put some of the marinades aside. Apply little melted butter to every piece of chicken using a pastry brush.

6. Cook chicken for 20 minutes at 350°F, often basting with the marinade you set beforehand. If you want crispy brown skin and fully cooked chicken with clear juices (an internal temperature of 165°F), you'll need to bake the chicken for an additional 15-25 minute.

7. If you are preparing a combination of chicken parts, remember that the breasts, depending on their size, may be done cooking before the thighs.

8. Chicken should be allowed to rest:

9. Take the chicken out of the oven and rest it for ten minutes with foil over it.

10. The chicken's natural fluids should be saved and served with the dish.

11. The juices from the pan should be poured into a serving basin. Remove the top layer of fat with a tbsp (save the fat for cooking later, or discard, but do not discard down the drain, or it will solidify and clog your drain).

12. The chicken can be served with the fluids on the side or drizzled lightly over the top.

13. You may eat it on its own, or you can pair it with mashed potatoes, angel hair pasta, steaming rice, or buttered noodles.

CRISPY DUCK PANCAKES

Prep: 10 minutes

Cook: 30 minutes

Ingredients

- ½ cucumber, cut into thin matchsticks small bunch of spring onions, shredded

For the duck
- 1 tbsp honey
- 1 tsp Chinese five-spice powder
- 2 duck breasts
- For the plum sauce
- 5 plums, halved and stoned
- 50ml agave syrup
- 1 tbsp soy sauce
- ½ tsp Chinese five-spice powder
- For the pancakes
- 150g plain flour

Method

rapeseed oil for brushing

1. Set the oven temperature up to 180 degrees Fahrenheit (160 degrees Celsius with the fan on) and 4 inches of gas. Honey and five-spice powder should be mixed in a basin, and then the mixture should be brushed all over the duck. Put in a roasting pan and bake at 400° for 25-30 minutes, or until browned. Wait 10 minutes, then thinly slice the skin and shred the flesh.

2. Prepare the plum sauce while the duck is in the oven by combining all of the sauce's components in a saucepan and simmering them over low heat for 15 minutes and the sauce has thickened. Smooth everything out using a stick blender.

3. Mix the flour, 125 ml of the hot water, and a pinch of salt together in a bowl until a dough forms while the sauce is simmering. Once it's cooled enough to handle, knead it for five to ten minutes. Cut it into 10 equal piece and roll every ball out as thin as you can. Oil a frying pan and cook the pancakes for 20 seconds on every side over medium heat or until set but not browned.

4. Use some plum sauce to top off a pancake. Shredded duck, cucumber, and spring onions are the finishing touches.

SESAME CHICKEN

Prep Time: 20 minutes

Cook Time: 20 minutes

Ingredients

For the chicken

- 1 1/2 lbs boneless skinless chicken breasts cut into
- 1-inch pieces Two eggs beaten
- salt and pepper as needed
- 1/2 cup of all-purpose flour
- 1/2 cup of cornstarch
- oil for frying

For the sauce

- 1 tsp vegetable oil
- 1 tsp minced fresh garlic
- 1/4 cup of honey
- 1/3 cup of soy sauce
- 1/2 cup of ketchup
- 3 tbsp brown sugar
- 2 tbsp rice vinegar
- 1 tbsp toasted sesame oil
- 2 tsp cornstarch
- 2 tbsp sesame seeds
- 2 tbsp sliced green onions

Instructions

1. Crack the egg into a bowl and season with salt & pepper. Mix by stirring

2. Put the flour and half a cup of cornstarch in a wide dish. Combining ingredients requires a good stir.

3. To bread the chicken, first, dips it in the egg mixture and then in the flour. Do the same with the remaining chicken.

4. To fry, heat 3 inche of oil to 350 degree Fahrenheit in a deep pan.

5. Put seven or eight chicken breasts in the skillet. For best results, cook for 5 minutes or until golden and crisp. For the remaining chicken, just keep going.

6. Towel-dry the chicken after it has been cooked.

7. Honey, soy sauce, ketchup, brown sugar, rice vinegar, sesame oil, and 2 tbsp of cornstarch should be mixed together in a bowl while the chicken cooks.

8. In a large pan, melt the tsp of butter over medium heat. Cook the garlic for 30 second after adding it. Then, stir in the honey sauce ingredients and reduce to a simmer. Leave it to simmer for three to four minutes or until it reverses the desired thickness.

9. Toss the crispy chicken with the sauce in the pan to coat. Serve with a garnish of green onions and sesame seeds.

KUNG PAO CHICKEN

Prep: 30 minutes

Cook: 30 minutes

Ingredients

- 2 tbsp cornstarch dissolved
- 2 tbsp white wine, divided
- 2 tbsp soy sauce, divided
- 2 tbsp sesame oil, divided
- 1 pound skinless, boneless chicken breast halves
- 1-ounce hot chile paste
- 2 tsp brown sugar
- 1 tsp distilled white vinegar
- 1 (8 ounces) can of water chestnuts
- 4 ounces chopped peanuts
- 4 green onions, chopped

Instructions

1. Put some cornstarch and water in a cup. Reserved for later use.

2. In a large glass bowl, whisk together the wine, soy sauce, sesame oil, and the cornstarch/water combination. Throw in the chicken and stir to coat. Refrigerate the dish for at least 30 minutes covered.

3. In a bowl, whisk together the remaining 1 tbsp of wine, 1 tbsp of soy sauce, 1 tbsp of sesame oil, and the remaining cornstarch/water combination. Add the chile paste, brown sugar, and vinegar and whisk to mix. Mix in some water chestnuts, peanuts, green onions, and garlic.

4. Put the water chestnut mixture in a medium-sized skillet. Slowly reheat over low to medium heat until fragrant.

5. In the meantime, drain the marinade from the chicken. Stir often over medium heat and cook until chicken is no longer pink in the middle and the juices run clear about 9-10 minutes.

6. Simmer the chicken with the water chestnut mixture in the same pan. Reduce the heat and let the mixture simmer to thicken the sauce.

THE BEST GENERAL TSO CHICKEN RECIPE

Prep: 10 minutes

Cook: 20 minutes

Ingredients

For the Marinade:

- 1 large egg white
- 2 tbsp Chinese dark soy sauce
- 2 tbsp Shaoxing wine
- 2 tbsp 80-proof vodka
- 3 tbsp cornstarch
- 1/4 tsp baking soda
- 1 pound boneless, skinless chicken thighs

For the Dry Coating:

- 1/2 cup of all-purpose flour
- 1/2 cup of cornstarch
- 1/2 tsp baking powder
- 1/2 tsp kosher salt

To Fry Chicken:

- 1 1/2 quarts peanut, vegetable, or canola oil for deep frying

For the Sauce and to Finish

- 4 tbsp granulated sugar
- 3 tbsp homemade or store-bought low-sodium chicken stock
- 3 tbsp dark soy sauce
- 2 tbsp Shaoxing wine
- 2 tbsp Chinese rice vinegar or distilled white vinegar

- 1 tbsp cornstarch
- 2 tsp peanut, vegetable, or canola oil
- 2 tsp minced garlic
- 2 tsp minced fresh ginger
- 2 tsp minced scallion bottoms
- 1 tsp (5ml) toasted sesame oil
- 8 small dried red Chinese
- 1 cup of loosely packed steamed white rice

Directions

1. In a large basin, beat the egg whites until they are somewhat frothy and can be broken down. This will be the marinade. Whisk in the wine, vodka, and soy sauce. In a separate dish, save half of the marinade. To the big basin, sift the cornstarch and then whisk in the baking soda until well mixed. Prepare the coating by adding the chicken to a big bowl and turning it with your fingers. Wrap it in plastic and set it away.

2. Dry Coat That Is. Stir together the dry ingredients (flour, cornstarch, baking powder, and salt) in a large basin. Stir with a whisk until the mixture is smooth. Whisk in the marinade you set up until the mixture resembles a coarse meal. Reserved for later use.

3. If you want to fry some chicken, do the following: Adjust the burner to keep oil at 350F (177C) and fill a big wok or Dutch oven with 1 1/2 quarts of peanut, vegetable, or canola oil.

4. Remove chicken from marinade and add to dry coating mixture, one piece at a time, tossing after every addition. When all the chicken has been put to the dry coating, give it a good toss while pressing the coating into the chicken with your hands to ensure a good bond.

5. Carefully lower every piece of chicken into the heated oil after shaking off any extra coating (do not drop it). Once all of the chicken has been added, cook for 4 minutes,

occasionally stirring with long chopsticks or a metal spider and adjusting the heat so that the chicken remains between 325 and 375 degrees Fahrenheit (163 and 191 degrees Celsius) until it is well cooked and extremely crispy. Place the chicken in a basin lined with paper towels to absorb any excess oil. When the oil is cold, pour it through a fine-mesh strainer into a large heat-safe basin.

6. In a bowl, whisk together the sugar, chicken stock, soy sauce, wine, vinegar, cornstarch, and sesame oil until the cornstarch is dissolved and there are no lumps. Reserved for later use.

7. Over medium heat, in a wok or big pan, mix the oil, garlic, ginger, chopped scallions, and red chilies. During this time, the veggies should become fragrant and soft without browning. Finally, add the sauce mixture to the wok and give it a good stir, being sure to get any sugar or starch stuck to the bottom of the bowl. To thicken the sauce, bring it to a boil and constantly whisk for 1 minute. Toss in some sliced scallions.

8. Toss the chicken in the sauce, using a wok spatula or a silicone spatula to fold and turn the piece, so they are evenly coated with the sauce. White rice should be served right away.

ORANGE CHICKEN STIR FRY

Prep: 10 minutes

Cook: 35 minutes

Ingredients

- 1 cup of orange juice
- 1 tbsp grated orange zest
- ¼ cup of soy sauce
- 1 tsp salt
- 3 cloves garlic, chopped
- 1 tbsp brown sugar
- 3 tbsp vegetable oil
- 4 skinless, boneless chicken breast
- 2 tbsp all-purpose flour
- 1 cup of bean sprouts (Optional)
- 1 (6 ounces) package of crispy chow mein noodles

Instructions

1. Mix together the orange juice, soy sauce, salt, orange zest, garlic, and brown sugar in a small bowl. Be sure to mix thoroughly.

2. Oil heated in a big pan over medium heat. Add chicken once the oil has begun to bubble. Seven to ten minutes of sautéing should be plenty to ensure that the interior is fully done.

3. Cook the chicken with the orange sauce mixture until the sauce bubbles. If you want a thicker sauce, add flour a little at a time. When the noodles are done, toss in the bean sprouts and simmer for an additional minute.

CASHEW CHICKEN

Total Time: 30 Minutes

Ingredients

- ¾ cup of roasted, unsalted cashews
- ¼ cup of water
- 2 tsp cornstarch
- 4 tbsp hoisin sauce, best quality such as Kikkoman
- 1½ pounds boneless, skinless chicken breasts
- ½ tsp salt
- ¼ tsp freshly ground black pepper
- 2 tbsp vegetable oil
- 6 medium garlic cloves, minced
- 8 scallions with white and green parts separated
- 2 tbsp rice vinegar
- ¼ tsp Asian sesame oil

Instructions

1. Set on the oven to 350 degrees Fahrenheit.
2. Spread the cashews out in a single layer on a baking sheet. The toasting process takes about 5 minutes in the oven or until the bread is aromatic. Put them aside; the cooling process will make them crispier.
3. Make the sauce by combining the water, cornstarch, hoisin sauce, and soy sauce in a small dish and whisking until smooth. Putting aside.
4. Prepare a big basin for the chicken pieces. Season with salt and pepper and stir to mix.
5. One tbsp of the vegetable oil should be heated over high heat until extremely hot in a big, nonstick pan. Stir-fry half of the chicken for 3 minutes, or until browned but not fully done. Put it onto a plate.

6. Place the last tbsp of oil in the pan and add the remaining chicken, garlic, and scallion whites. About 3 minutes should be enough time for the chicken to color in the pan without being fully cooked. The chicken from the first batch should be put back into the pan. Reduce heat to medium and add rice vinegar; simmer for 30 seconds, or until almost completely evaporated.

7. Toss the chicken with the sauce mixture and simmer for another minute. Take it out of the oven. Add the scallion greens, cashews, and sesame oil and stir. It's time to start serving now.

SWEET AND SOUR CHICKEN RECIPE

Time: 25 minutes

Cook time: 1 hour

Ingredients

- 2 1/2 lbs boneless chicken breast salt and pepper
- 1 cup of cornstarch
- 3 eggs, lightly beaten
- 1/4 cup of vegetable oil
- 1 cup of sugar
- 6 tbsp ketchup
- 3/4 cup of apple cider vinegar
- 1 1/2 tbsp soy sauce
- 1 1/2 tsp garlic powder

Instructions

1. Shred the chicken into manageable pieces. Add some salt and pepper for flavor.

2. Have a 325-degree Fahrenheit oven ready.

3. Cornstarch should be placed in a wide, shallow dish. Separate an egg dish for the eggs. Prepare the oil by heating it in a skillet over moderate heat. Dredge the chicken in the cornstarch, then dip it in the egg, working in batches if necessary. Brown on all sides by adding to the heated oil. You can produce a crispy surface by browning the chicken, but there's no need to cook it all the way through. Repeat with the entire chicken, transferring it to a 9-by- 13-inch baking dish every time.

4. Sugar, ketchup, cider vinegar, soy sauce, garlic powder, and a pinch of salt should be mixed together in a basin. Coat the chicken with the sauce and serve.

5. After an hour in the oven, stirring once every 15 minutes, the chicken should be done. Cooked rice is recommended.

EASY CHICKEN CURRY

Prep time: 5 minutes

Cook time: 25 minutes

Ingredients

- 2 tbsp sunflower oil
- 1 onion, thinly sliced
- 2 garlic cloves, crushed
- a thumb-sized piece of ginger, grated
- 6 chicken thighs, boneless and skinless
- 3 tbsp medium spice paste
- 400g can of chopped tomatoes
- 100g Greek yogurt
- 1 small bunch of coriander, leaves chopped
- 50g ground almonds
- naan bread or cooked basmati rice, to serve

Method

1. Oil should be heated over medium heat in a flameproof casserole dish or big frying pan. Put in the onion and a good amount of salt, and cook for 8 to 10 minutes, or until the onion is golden brown and sticky. Sauté for a further minute after adding the garlic and ginger.

2. You'll need to cut the chicken into 3-centimeter cubes, put them in the pan, and cook them for 5 minutes before adding the spice paste, tomatoes, and 250 ml of water. Bring to a boil, decrease the heat to low, and simmer, uncovered, for 25 to 30 minutes, or until thick and rich. Mix in the yogurt, coriander, and ground almonds, then season as needed. Serve over hot naan or fluffy basmati rice.

SHRIMP WITH LOBSTER SAUCE

Prep time: 10 minutes

Cook time: 15 minutes

Ingredients

- 12 oz raw large shrimp, shelled and deveined salt and sugar as needed
- 2 tbsp vegetable oil
- 1 inch piece of ginger, peeled
- 2 cloves garlic, thinly sliced
- 1/3 cup of chicken broth
- 1/2 tbsp Shaoxing Chinese cooking wine,
- 3/4 cup of store-bought frozen vegetables, peas, and carrots
- 3 dashes of white pepper
- 1/2 tbsp light soy sauce
- 1 tbsp corn starch
- 2 tbsp water
- 1 egg white, lightly beaten

Instructions

1. Sprinkle the shrimp with a little bit of salt and sugar and cook until done.

2. Get the oil hot in a wok over medium heat. Then, when the oil is heated, throw in the ginger and garlic. Put in a wok and heat for 2 minutes, or until fragrant.

3. Put the shrimp in the wok and stir-fry until they are just opaque on the surface, about halfway through cooking. Chicken broth and Chinese cooking wine should be added now. Turn up the heat and let it boil.

4. The frozen veggies should be added and mixed together. Season as needed with white pepper, soy sauce, salt, and sugar.

5. To make the cornstarch mixture, just mix the cornstarch and water and stir until smooth. While constantly stirring, slowly add the cornstarch mixture to the boiling chicken stock.

6. Then, with chopsticks, stir three times while swirling in the beaten egg as it returns to a boil. Take off the heat as soon as the egg white begins to form silky strands.

7. Spread out on a serving platter. This dish pairs especially well with hot rice.

SALT AND PEPPER SQUID

Prep: 20 minutes

Cook: 20 minutes

Ingredients

- 1 1/2 pounds squid
- 1 tbsp Shaoxing wine
- 1/2 tsp sesame oil
- 5 cups of vegetable oil
- 1/2 cup of all-purpose flour
- 1/2 cup of semolina flour
- 1/3 cup of plain cornmeal
- 1 tsp salt
- 1/2 tsp white pepper
- 2 long hot green peppers
- 5 cloves garlic
- 2 tsp ginger

Instructions

1. The squid must be prepared first. Run some cold water over it to clean it. Make a single incision through the body, reserving a quarter of an inch of the hood, and the tentacles will come out in one piece. These may be made into bite-sized portions by slicing the squid in half lengthwise if you're using bigger squid. If you want your calamari to cook evenly, it's crucial that every piece is around the same size. After washing the squid in a colander, remove the pieces and place them in a basin.

2. Mix the Shaoxing wine and sesame oil, then use the mixture to marinate the squid. Gently toss and put away.

3. Be sure to add enough oil to a medium-deep pot so that it comes about four inches up the edge of the pot. Bring the oil to heat temperature of 325 degrees.

4. Start working on the dry ingredients while the oil heats. Blend the cornmeal, all-purpose flour, semolina flour, salt, and white pepper in a medium bowl. Putting aside.

5. As soon as the oil is hot enough, you may begin dredging the squid. Pursue the calamari in little, fist-sized chunks. After removing excess moisture, dredge the squid in the dry ingredients.

6. Toss the calamari into the heated oil using a long-handled strainer or slotted spoon. Calamari pieces should be gently tossed back and forth. Leave them in the pan for 2–2 1/2 minutes, or until the outside is golden brown. Take out all the calamari and drain it on a platter lined with paper towels. if you're able to endure the heat, try a piece of calamari and see how salty it is. As soon as they come out of the fryer, salt as needed. However, once the squid has been cooked, it must be seasoned with freshly cracked white pepper. Fry the squid in tiny batches, sprinkling every batch with white pepper, until it is fully cooked.

7. The fried squid will now be stir-fried. Preheat a wok over moderate heat. One spoonful of oil from a vegetable source. Put the ginger into the oil and let it cook. When the onion has cooked for around 20 seconds, add the garlic. Quickly move the garlic about the wok to prevent it from burning. Add the peppers after the garlic has turned a golden brown hue. Fry for another 30 seconds, stirring constantly.

8. After approximately a minute of stir-frying in the fragrant mixture, add the squid to the pan. Serve over white rice right away. Don't throw away the fried bits of garlic and pepper!

KUNG PAO SHRIMP

Time: 15 minutes

Ingredients

- 1 lb peeled and deveined medium shrimp
- 2 tbsp Shaoxing wine or dry sherry
- 2 tsp cornstarch
- Salt
- 2 tbsp granulated sugar
- 3 tbsp soy sauce
- 2 tbsp Chinkiang vinegar
- ½ tsp Sichuan peppercorns, coarsely ground, plus more as need
- 1 red or orange bell pepper
- 5 garlic cloves
- ¼ cup of neutral oil, such as grapeseed
- ½ cup of unsalted roasted peanuts
- ¾ cup of small dried red chiles
- 3 large scallions, cut into 1/2-inch lengths

Preparation

1. To ensure the shrimp are equally coated, mix 1 tsp of cornstarch, a bit of salt, and the Shaoxing wine in a dish. Leave to rest while you get the other stuff ready.

2. Sugar, soy sauce, vinegar, Sichuan pepper, and the remaining 1 tsp of cornstarch should be mixed together in a separate basin. Peel the garlic cloves and cut them into thin slice. Put all the ingredients within the easy recovery of the burner.

3. 15 seconds over medium heat is all it takes to heat the oil in a wok or big skillet. Put in the peanuts and swirl them about for 30-60 seconds, or until they start to

become a little brown. Pepper and garlic should be added, along with a pinch of salt. Cook, constantly stirring, for approximately 30 seconds, or until the pepper is brilliant and the garlic is beginning to become translucent. Chilli peppers and their marinade should be added; then, the shrimp should be stirred in. Toss the shrimp every so often while cooking for 2 to 3 minutes or until they are curled and barely opaque.

4. Once the scallions have been stirred for around 15 seconds, they should be glossy and ready to receive the sauce. Stirring constantly, bring to a boil, and continue cooking for 1 minute, or until the sauce has thickened and coated the food well. A splash of water and a scrape of the pan might help loosen any starchy sauce that has adhered to the bottom of the pan. Put a little in your mouth and see whether you want more Sichuan pepper. Put it on a platter right away, so it stays hot when served.

FISH WITH SPICY BEAN SAUCE

Prep:20 minutes

Cook:15 minutes

Ingredients

- 1 large fish filet
- ¼ cup of shiitake mushrooms
- ¼ cup of carrot (finely chopped)
- ¼ cup of red pepper (finely chopped)
- ¼ cup of onion (finely chopped)
- ¼ cup of ground pork (optional)
- 1 tbsp water
- 1 tbsp cornstarch
- 1 tbsp Shaoxing wine
- 1 tbsp spicy bean sauce (doubanjiang)
- 1 tsp hoisin sauce
- 1/2 tsp sesame oil
- 1/2 tsp sugar
- 1/8 tsp Ground white pepper
- Oil
- 1 clove of garlic (minced)
- 1/2 cup of water
- 2 tsp cilantro
- 1 tbsp scallions

Instructions

1. Cook the fish in a steamer, then drain and serve. If you want to learn more about how to prepare your fish, check out this recipe for Cantonese Steamed Fish.

2. It's a good idea to have the veggies and pork ready to cook while the fish is steaming. Create a slurry by combining the 1 tbsp of water and the cornstarch. In a small bowl,

mix the Shaoxing wine, bean sauce, hoisin sauce, sesame oil, sugar, and white pepper.

3. Stir-fry garlic and onions in 1 tbsp of oil in a hot wok. After one minute of stirring, throw in the remaining produce and meat. Keep stirring for one more minute. To the sauce you've just made, add the other ingredients and mix well. Bring your water to a low simmer and add it.

4. Use the cornstarch slurry to thicken the sauce until it coats a spoon. The consistency adjusted by adding more water or slurry, respectively. Finish the sauce by whisking in a tsp of oil, then serving it on cooked fish. Cilantro and scallion can be used as a garnish, and the dish should be served right away.

FISH WITH BLACK BEAN SAUCE

Prep Time: 15 minutes

Cook time: 15 minutes

Ingredients

- 500g fish fillet, cut into medium-sized cubes
- 12 pcs small blocks of fried tofu
- One large green capsicum/bell pepper, sliced
- 2 tbsp salted black beans
- 2 tbsp black bean sauce
- 1 tbsp soy sauce
- 1/2 tsp sugar
- 1 cup of water
- 1/2 cup of cornstarch
- 4 cloves garlic, minced
- 1 thumb-sized ginger, minced
- 1 shallot, minced
- fish sauce or sea salt
- freshly ground black pepper oil

Instructions

1. Put some cornstarch on a dish and use it to gently coat the fish.

2. It takes around 2 to 3 minutes on every side to shallow fried fish in hot oil in a wok until it is golden brown and flaky.

3. When cooking fish, use the same pan to sauté the garlic, shallot, and ginger.

4. Put in some green bell pepper and stir-fry for a minute. Toss in some fish and tofu.

5. Cook the fish in a pot with water, black bean sauce, soy
   sauce, sugar, and black beans until the sauce is thick,
   about 5 minutes. Add some cornstarch slurry to the sauce
   if it needs thickening.

6. Fish sauce and freshly ground black pepper make a great
   seasoning combination.

SHANGHAI SHRIMP STIR-FRY

Ready 25 minutes

Servings 4

Ingredients

- 1 pound Shrimp
- 1 cup of Peanut oil
- 2 whole Scallions
- 3 slices of Fresh ginger
- 1 tbsp Shaoxing wine
- 0.5 cup of Chicken Stock
- 1 tsp Sugar
- 0.25 tsp Chinese black vinegar
- 1 tsp Toasted sesame oil
- 0.25 tsp Salt

Instructions

1. At first cook the shrimp. Remove the legs and the pointed tip of the head using kitchen shears. The shrimp's vein may be removed with a toothpick by gently prying it out of the shell (picture below). The shrimp should be washed in cold water, drained, and patted dry using a paper towel.

2. Oil heated in a wok until it begins to smoke over high heat. Fry the shrimp gently for around 5-10 seconds per batch, lowering them carefully into the oil in two stages. Translucency in the shrimp will rapidly disappear. Quickly transfer them to a metal strainer to return any accumulated oil to the pan. Do not eat the shrimp just yet.

3. Turn the heat back on and wait for the oil to smoke again. Fry the shrimp for another 5-10 seconds, lowering them into the oil in two batches. Overflying can dry out the shrimp, so adjust the cooking time accordingly.

4. Take the wok from the heat and pour all except about 1 tbsp of the oil into a heat-safe basin. The white of the scallions and the ginger should be added at this point, and the heat should be reduced to low. Let it simmer for 2 minutes or until the aroma is pleasantly strong. To the chicken broth, Shaoxing wine, sugar, and vinegar, add the ingredients. Boost the temperature until the liquid reverses a simmer. Put in a pot and stir for 30 seconds.

5. The scallions and ginger may now be removed from the wok, or they can be left in there if desired. At last, return the shrimp to the skillet and drizzle in the sesame oil. Cook for another 5-10 seconds, or until the shrimp are completely covered in the sauce during the stir-frying process. As needed, add salt and serve.

CASHEW SHRIMP STIR-FRY

Prep: 2 hours 30 minutes

Cook: 5 minutes

Ingredients

- 8 oz. medium shrimp 225g, peeled and deveined
- 1 1/4 tsp sugar divided
- 1/8 tsp baking soda
- 1/4 cup of water
- 1/2 tsp sesame oil
- 1 tsp cornstarch
- salt and white pepper
- 4 stalks celery
- 1/2 red bell pepper sliced
- 1 1/2 tbsp oil
- 2 slices of ginger minced
- 1 scallion chopped
- 2 tsp oyster sauce
- 3/4 cup of cashews

Instructions

1. To begin, clean and cook the shrimp. For two minutes, gently toss the shrimp in a mixture of 1 tsp sugar, baking soda, and 1/4 cup of water. After covering and chilling for 2 hours, rinse under cold running water for 5 minutes to remove any traces of sugar and baking soda. Use a paper towel to dry the shrimp completely. While you're getting the other ingredients ready, marinate the shrimp in 1/2 tsp of sesame oil, 1 tsp of cornstarch, 1/4 tsp of salt, and a bit of white pepper.

2. To prevent overcooking the shrimp in the little amount of time it takes to put this dish together, blanch the celery

and red bell pepper now. Drop the celery and red bell pepper into boiling water. The veggies should be drained after 30 seconds and then shocked in cold water. Rinse well and leave aside.

3. Aim for medium heat in a wok and add 1 1/2 tsp of oil. For the final minute of cooking, add the minced ginger and scallion. Then, place the shrimp in the pan and increase the heat to high. Add the blanched celery and red bell pepper after the shrimp have just started to turn pink, along with the remaining 1/4 tsp sugar, the oyster sauce, and the cashews. Stir the ingredients together and season with salt and white pepper as needed. Serve.

CREAMY GARLIC SCALLOPS

Prep: 5 minutes

Cook: 5 minutes

Ingredients

- 2 tbsp olive oil
- 1 1/4 pounds (600 grams) of scallops
- 2 tbsp unsalted butter, divided
- 4-5 large garlic cloves, minced
- Salt and fresh ground black pepper
- 1/4 cup of dry white wine or broth (optional)
- 1 cup of heavy cream
- 1 tbsp lemon juice
- 1/4 cup of chopped parsley

Instructions

1. Thaw frozen scallops in cold water. If the scallops still have their side muscle attached, cut it off. You should use a lot of paper towels to dry off.

2. Put the olive oil in a big pan or skillet and turn the heat to medium-high, so it begins to sizzle. Take the scallops in the pan in a single layer (work in batches if needed).

3. Fry in oil until a golden crust develops on one side (about 2 minutes), season with salt and pepper as needed, then turn to cook for another 2 minutes, until crisp, browned, and fully done (opaque). Put on a dish and stop cooking in the skillet.

4. In the same pan, the scallops were cooked in, melt 2 tbsp of butter and use a wooden spoon to scrape off any browned parts. Sauté the garlic until it's fragrant. Add the wine or broth and boil for 2 minutes, or until the wine is reduced by half. Simmer the cream until it has thickened a little, then add it.

5. Turn off the heat and whisk in the lemon juice before returning the scallops to the pan to reheat and garnish with the parsley.

6. Serve with steamed veggies, rice, pasta, or garlic bread (cauliflower, broccoli, zucchini noodles).

CANTONESE STYLE LOBSTER

Prep: 20 minutes

Cook: 20 minutes

Ingredients

- 2 small (1 pound) fresh live lobsters
- ⅓ cup of peanut oil, divided
- 1 clove of garlic, crushed
- 1 slice fresh ginger root, minced
- 6 ounces lean ground pork
- 1 cup of chicken broth
- 1 tbsp cooking sherry
- 1 tbsp soy sauce
- 1 tbsp cornstarch
- 1 tsp brown sugar
- 2 eggs, beaten
- 3 green onions, chopped

Instructions

1. Hold the lobster upside down while you wash it. A small aperture may be found at the base of the tail; insert a long skewer inside to drain any remaining urine from the animal's body before cracking off the tail, chopping it into small pieces, and cracking the claws in two. Throw in the lobster's body as well if you know how to eat it.

2. In a large, deep pan, melt half of the peanut oil over moderate heat. Crush some garlic and throw it in the pan for a minute or so. Toss the lobster in and sauté for 4 to 5 minutes, or until cooked through. Take the garlicky lobster combination and put it on a plate.

3. Preheat the pan with the remaining oil. As soon as the pork is no longer pink, stir in the minced ginger

and continue cooking. Chicken broth should be added, and the dish should be brought to a boil while being stirred frequently. Whisk together the sherry, soy sauce, cornstarch, and brown sugar in a small bowl. Stir in the sherry mixture, and cook for another minute or two, until the sauce has thickened and is mostly clear.

4. Removed the heat and add the green onions. Add the beaten eggs a bit at a time, stirring constantly, to the ingredients in the pan. After that, put the lobster back in the pan and let it simmer for a few minutes to let the flavors mingle. Put in a serving dish and cover to rest for a few minutes. Eat it with some steaming rice and relish it because you earned it.

MOO SHU SHRIMP

Prep Time: 25 minutes

Cook time: 15 minutes

Ingredients

- 1/2 pound shrimp peeled, deveined
- 1/8 tsp sea salt
- 1 tsp rice wine
- 2 tsp cornstarch
- 3 tbsp oil
- 2 large eggs
- 12 ounces napa cabbage cut into thin shreds
- 1 carrot peeled, shredded
- 1/2 red bell pepper cut
- 6 dried shitake mushrooms rehydrated
- 1/3 cup of rehydrated wood ear mushrooms cut into bite-size pieces
- 1 tbsp soy sauce
- 1 tbsp rice wine
- 1 tbsp sesame oil
- 2 scallions cut into 1" lengths

Instructions

1. While the remainder of the dish is being prepared, mix the shrimp with the salt, rice wine, and cornstarch in a medium bowl.

2. Bring 1 tbsp of oil to temperature in a pan that won't stick. Stir-fry the shiitake and wood ear mushrooms until they are cooked through, then add the napa cabbage, carrot, pepper, and other vegetables. Put the veg in a big basin. Purge the wok with water.

3. Put 1 tbsp of oil into the wok and let it heat up. After the eggs have been scrambled and are fully cooked, they should be added to a bowl containing previously prepared veggies.

4. In a pan, warm the extra tbsp of oil. Stir in shrimp and cook until opaque throughout, about 3 minutes.

5. Add the cooked eggs and veggies back into the wok and stir in the shrimp. Toss in the soy sauce, rice wine, and sesame oil. Toss in the scallions.

6. Chinese flour tortillas or Mandarin pancakes can be served alongside hoisin sauce.

STIR-FRIED MIXED VEGETABLES

Prep: 10min

Cook: 10 min

Ingredients

- 2 tbsp vegetable oil
- 2 garlic cloves, crushed
- 1 medium brown onion, halved, sliced
- 1 long red chili, sliced into rounds
- 1/2 small head cauliflower cut
- 2 green onions, trimmed, cut into 6cm lengths
- 1 medium carrot, peeled, scored along the edge with a knife, sliced into rounds
- 1/2 cup of Massel chicken-style liquid stock
- 1 1/2 tsp cornflour
- 1/2 small Chinese cabbage (wombok), thickly sliced

Instructions

1. Oil should be heated in a deep frying pan or wok over medium heat. Put in some onions, garlic, and peppers. Do the stir-frying for 2 minutes or until the onion is softened. Raise the temperature to high. Throw in some cauliflower, green onion, and a carrot. Carrots should be cooked in a stir-fry for around three minutes.

2. In a liquid measuring cup, mix 1/4 cup of hot water with cornstarch. The work will benefit from the addition of the stock and cornflour combination, for 2 minutes, or until the sauce boils and thickens, stir-fry over high heat.

Incorporate some cabbage. Cook for 1 minute, or until barely wilted, in a stir-fry. Add some salt and pepper for flavor. It's time to start serving now.

EGG FOO YOUNG (CHINESE OMELETTE)

Prep: 10 minutes

Cook: 15 minutes

Ingredients

- 4 tsp cornflour corn starch
- 1 1/2 tbsp light soy sauce
- 2 tsp Oyster Sauce
- 1 tbsp Chinese Cooking Wine
- 1/2 tsp sesame oil
- 1 cup of / 250 ml water
- Dash of white pepper

OMELETTE:

- 6 eggs
- 2 cups of bean sprouts
- 4 shallots/green onions, white part only, sliced
- Salt and white pepper
- 2 tbsp vegetable oil
- 1 tsp sesame oil
- 1 garlic clove, finely chopped
- 1/2 tsp EVERY soy sauce and Oyster Sauce
- 1/4 tsp sugar
- Dash of sesame oil

GARNISH (OPTIONAL):

- Sesame seeds, sliced green onion

Instructions

1. Mix the cornstarch and soy sauce. So, throw in the rest of the stuff.

2. The mixture should be poured into a saucepan and heated over medium heat. Raise the heat until it just barely simmers, stirring often. Hold at a low boil for 1 minute, or until the sauce reverses a thin syrup consistency. Take off the heat and put it to the side.

3. TABLET or MICROWAVE? Set the microwave to high and cook for 1 1/2 minutes. After 1 minute and a half in the microwave, stir vigorously and check the consistency. Again, stir the ingredients together thoroughly.

4. Mix all of the remaining ingredients with the pork in a bowl. Mix using a fork.

5. Beat eggs in a bowl.

6. Season with salt and pepper, and add beansprouts, green onions, pork, or prawns. Add raw pork by crumbling it with your fingertips (see video). Totally mix the ingredients.

7. Using a nonstick pan, heat half a tbsp of vegetable oil and a sprinkle of sesame oil over medium heat. Saute the garlic for 10 seconds before pushing it to the center of the pan.

8. Dollop in a quarter of the mixture. Form a spherical object by pushing in on its edges with a spatular.

9. After 1 1/2 minutes, rotate and cook for another minute until the opposite side is lightly brown. In that time, the uncooked meat will be fully cooked. It's best to use 2 pans so you may create 4 omelets with the leftover egg.

10. Arrange the omelet on a plate by sliding it there. To be used with sauce. Add sesame seeds and green onions, if using.

11. Accompany with steamed rice and your preferred veggies. If you want to use the sauce to coat the rice and vegetables, you'll need to make twice as much.

CHINESE DRY-SAUTEED STRING BEANS

Ready in: 20 minutes

Ingredients

- 1lb green beans, fresh and dry
- 1 tbsp garlic, minced
- 1 tbsp ginger, minced
- 2 callions, minced
- 1/2 tsp chili paste with garlic
- 1/2 tsp chili paste, sriracha
- 1 tbsp soy sauce
- 1/2 tsp sugar
- 1/4 tsp salt pepper
- 2 tbsp peanut oil or
- 2 tbsp vegetable oil, divided

Directions

1. In a wok, heat 1 tbsp of oil over moderate heat. If you don't use a wok and get the oil hot beforehand, this won't turn out. Put in the green beans (watch out for the splatters!) and stir-fry them until they are a little puckered and browned (about 6-8 minutes).

2. Green beans can be drained in a colander.

3. Stir sauté the ginger, garlic, and scallions in the remaining 1 T of oil for a minute. Fry for one minute with chili sauce and siracha. Put in the beans and season with sugar, salt, pepper, and soy sauce.

4. To accompany rice.

SALT AND PEPPER TOFU

Prep:20 minutes

Cook:15 minutes

Ingredients

- FOR THE TOFU BRINE:
- 14 ounces firm tofu
- 1/4 tsp garlic powder
- 1/2 tsp onion powder
- 1/2 tsp salt
- 1 tsp sugar
- 1 1/4 cups of warm water
- 1/2 tsp sesame oil
- 1 tsp Shaoxing wine

FOR THE TOFU SEASONING AND DREDGE:

- 3/4 tsp salt
- 3/4 tsp ground white pepper
- 1/4 tsp ground Sichuan Peppercorn
- 1/4 tsp sand ginger powder
- 2 tbsp all-purpose flour
- 2 tbsp cornstarch

FOR THE REST OF THE DISH:

- 4 tbsp vegetable oil
- 5 cloves garlic
- 1 long hot green pepper
- 1 shallot
- 1 scallion
- 1 tbsp cilantro chopped

Instructions

1. Cut the tofu into rectangles that are 1 1/2 inches (4 cm) long and 2 inches (5 cm) wide. Create the brine by combining the garlic powder, onion powder, salt, sugar, and warm water in a bowl and whisking to mix. Soak the tofu in the brine for at least an hour and up to two.

2. After 1–2 hours, remove all of the liquid from the tofu and let it drain for 5 minutes. Once more, drain the tofu and gently mix it with the sesame oil and Shaoxing wine.

3. Add the Sichuan peppercorn powder, crushed ginger powder, powdered white pepper, and salt to a bowl and mix well. Tofu will be coated with half of this salt and pepper spice mixture, and the other half will be used for the final wok toss.

4. Toss the tofu in an all-purpose flour and cornstarch mixture that has had half of the spice blend added. Toss the tofu with the remaining flour mixture and then flip it over. The batter-like coating will form on the surface of the damp tofu as it absorbs the dredging. If the mixture seems too watery, or if you want your tofu crispier, you may add a bit of extra cornstarch.

5. For 30 seconds, heat 4 tbsp of oil in a wok set over low heat. Put in some garlic. In this low heat setting, it should gently boil and sizzle without burning. Burnt garlic tastes unpleasant, so you'll want to wait. To ensure consistent cooking, stir the garlic around in the oil. To determine when it is ready, look for a light golden brown color.

6. Take it out of the wok with a slotted spoon or drain it through a fine-mesh strainer, but keep the oil there. Put the garlic on a paper towel-lined platter.

7. Oil should be heated in a wok over medium heat. Brown the tofu by placing it in a single layer in a wok and turning up the heat as necessary. Don't leave the oven unattended, or you'll burn the crust! Brown one side of the tofu and

then flip it over to brown the other. Put the tofu on a platter once it has finished cooking.

8. Coat the edges of the wok with the remaining oil and reserve the standing oil for further use.

9. Crank the heat to high on the stove. Stir-fry the shallots and long spicy green peppers for 15-30 seconds. Then, after about 30-60 seconds of gentle tossing, add the warmed tofu. Incorporate the fresh herbs and garlic chips. Keep throwing for the next minute and a half.

10. Season the tofu and aromatics with the remaining salt and pepper. The fried tofu will soak up the seasoning, giving it a more robust flavor. Toss again for 15 seconds, then transfer to a serving platter.

MAP TOFU

Prep: 10 minutes

Cook: 25 minutes

Ingredients

- ½ cup of oil
- 1-2 fresh Thai bird chili peppers
- 6-8 dried red chilies
- 2 tbsp Sichuan
- 3 tbsp ginger
- 3 tbsp garlic
- 8 ounces ground pork
- 1-2 tbsp spicy bean sauce
- 2/3 cup of low sodium chicken broth
- 1 pound silken tofu
- 1 1/2 tsp cornstarch
- 1/4 tsp sesame oil (optional)
- 1/4 tsp sugar (optional)
- 1 scallion (finely chopped)

Instructions

1. In the beginning, the chilies are toasted. If you have access to toasted chili oil, you may skip this step. Preheat a wok or a small pot on low heat. Add the fresh and dried peppers and a quarter cup of the oil. Make sure the peppers don't burn by stirring regularly and heating the mixture for about 5 minutes until aromatic. Removed off the heat and put it aside.

2. Over medium heat, bring the remaining 1/4 cup of oil to a shimmer in the wok. The ginger should be added. Just after the first minute is up, toss in the garlic. Turn the heat to high and add the ground pork after another minute

of frying. Shred the meat and fry it in small batches until it's done. Stir in the ground Sichuan peppercorns and cook for 15-30 seconds, keeping a close eye on them, so they don't burn and turn bitter.

3. Toss in the hot bean sauce and mix everything thoroughly. Put two to three cups of chicken stock in the pan and mix. Give it a minute or two to simmer. While that is going, get your tofu ready and add a quarter cup of water and your cornstarch in a small basin.

4. After combining the cornstarch and water, add it to your sauce and whisk to incorporate. Keep the heat on low and let it simmer until the sauce thickens. (Add some additional water or chicken stock if it becomes too thick.)

5. Then pour in the pepper-filled chili oil you previously prepared. When utilizing homemade chili oil, only use the oil that has settled to the bottom of the container because it is possible that you have already added salt to the oil. Oil should be added to the sauce before adding the tofu. Gently mix the tofu in the sauce using the spatula. Wait around five minutes before you serve. Toss in the scallions, sesame oil, and sugar (if using), and toss until the scallions are wilted.

6. Food tastes better in the summer because of the warmer weather. It's OK to serve food from the kitchen since it adds to the evening's ambiance. Enjoy!

7. If you'd like, you may sprinkle some Sichuan peppercorn powder on top before serving.

EGGPLANT WITH GARLIC SAUCE

Prep Time: 5 minutes

Cook time: 10 minutes

Ingredients

- 2–3 long Japanese
- 2 tbsp peanut oil
- 4 large peeled and minced cloves of garlic
- 1 tbsp ginger, peeled and minced
- 2–3 Chinese dried red chilis, chopped
- 4 scallions, finely chopped on the bias

For the sauce:

- 2 tbsp soy sauce
- 2 tsp granulated sugar
- 1 tbsp Chinkiang vinegar
- 1 tbsp Shaoxing wine or dry sherry
- 1 tsp sesame oil

Instructions

1. Take the sauce ingredient in a bowl and whisk them together.

2. Put the eggplant and 1 tbsp of the peanut oil into a large skillet and cook over medium heat. Cook in a wok for approximately 5 minutes, or until the outside is golden and the inside is soft.

3. After removing the eggplant from the pan, add the final tbsp of peanut oil. One minute into cooking, add the garlic, ginger, and red chilies.

4. Stir in the eggplant and scallions, then pour over the sauce and stir. The veggies should be stir-fried for 1 minute to ensure they are evenly covered.

5. Immediately remove from heat and serve over white or
   brown rice.

HUNAN TOFU VEGETABLE STIR-FRY

Prep time: 10 minutes

Cook time: 20 minutes

Ingredients

- For tofu
- 1 block of extra firm tofu drained
- 1 tbsp corn starch
- ½ tsp salt
- For stir-fry sauce
- ½ cup of vegetable broth
- 2 tbsp vegetarian oyster sauce
- 1 tbsp soy sauce
- 1 tbsp sambal oelek
- 2 tsp coconut sugar
- 2 tsp corn starch
- 1 tsp rice vinegar For stir-fry
- 3 cloves garlic minced
- 1 medium red bell pepper diced
- 1 cup of broccoli florets
- 6-8 baby corn halved lengthwise
- 0.5 oz dried wood ear mushrooms rehydrated

Instructions

1. To begin, cube your tofu so that it is easily snackable. Tofu, corn starch, and salt should be mixed in a medium-sized resealable plastic bag. Mix the tofu cubes with the coating by shaking the bag around.

2. 1 block of extra-firm tofu, 1 tbsp of corn starch, 1/2 tsp of salt. In a nonstick pan, heat 1 tbsp of neutral-tasting oil over medium heat. Put the tofu cubes in a single layer and

heat for about three minutes per side or until browned. Place aside.

3. Make the Hunan sauce while the tofu is in the oven. Put off using it for now.

4. Half a spoonful of oil should be added to the same pan. Put in the garlic and cook for approximately a minute, or until the aroma has developed.

5. THREE garlic clovers Sprinkle in some red pepper and broccoli. If you want your vegetables to be somewhat softer after cooking, give them another 3–4 minutes.

6. The ingredients are 1 red bell pepper and 1 cup of broccoli florets. Throw in some baby corn and black fungus now. Continue to sauté for an additional two to three minutes, or until vegetables are tender.

7. Baby corn (6-8) with dried wood ear mushrooms (0.5 ounces). Add the tofu and stir-fry sauce at the end. Raise the temperature to a low simmer and cook the mixture for a few minutes. When the sauce has thickened, it's ready to be served.

GREEN JADE VEGETABLES

Ready in: 15 minutes

Serves: 6

Ingredients

- 2 pounds (1 bunch) of broccoli
- 1 clove of garlic, minced
- 1 tbsp cornstarch
- 2 tbsp soy sauce
- 1/2 cup of water or vegetable stock
- 1/4 cup of vegetable oil
- 1/8 tsp salt
- 2 tbsp sherry

Instructions

1. Wash and peel the broccoli. Remove tops at an angle of 1/8 inch. In a bowl, mix cornstarch, soy sauce, and either chicken stock or water. Putting aside.

2. Prepare an extremely hot and dry wok or cast-iron skillet. First, drizzle oil over it, and then sprinkle salt on top. Add garlic and increase the heat to medium. The broccoli should be added when the onion is golden brown. Toss in the pan and stir for three minutes.

3. Quickly cover the pan after adding the sherry. Cover and set timer for 2 minutes.

4. Then, mix in the cornstarch slurry until the sauce has thickened.

FORTUNE COOKIES

servings: 6

Ingredients

- 1 egg white
- ⅛ tsp vanilla extract
- 1 pinch salt
- ¼ cup of unleveled all-purpose flour
- ¼ cup of white sugar

Instructions

1. Make sure your oven is preheated at 400 degrees F. Melt butter and use it to grease a baking pan. Preparing strips of paper that are 4 inches in length and 1/2 inch in width is ideal for writing down fortunes. Prepare 2 baking sheets by liberally greasing them.

2. Egg whites and vanilla extract should be whisked until frothy but not stiff. Mix the sifted dry ingredients (flour, salt, and sugar) with the beaten egg whites.

3. Drop by cupfuls onto one of the prepared cookie sheets, leaving at least 4 inches between every mound. The batter may be shifted into forms no larger than 3 inches in diameter by tilting the sheet. The batter should be as uniform and spherical as possible. Do not create too many since you need the cookie to be very hot to shape it, and once it cools, it will no longer be usable. Two or three to a sheet is a good place to start and then see how many you can complete.

4. Wait 5 minutes, or until the outside, 1/2 inch of the circle, is golden brown, if baking. You may expect the core to

keep its delicate color. Make the other sheet while the first is in the oven.

5. Take the cookie out of the oven and immediately flip it over with a large spatula, setting it down upside down on a wooden surface. Place the fortune towards the cookie's center and quickly fold it in half to reveal the message. A measuring cup may be used as a funnel if you lay the folded edge across the rim and draw the pointed edges down, one on the inside and one on the outside. Folded cookies can be stored in a muffin tray or egg carton to maintain their shape while they set in the fridge.

MANGO PUDDING

Prep Time: 7 minutes

Cook time: 8 minutes

Ingredients

- 2 medium Alphonso mangoes
- 3 tbsp raw sugar or add as required
- 2 tbsp finely chopped agar strands
- ⅓ cup of water
- 200 ml Coconut Milk

Instructions

1. At fast wash and peel two mangoes of medium size. Put them in the jar of your mixer or blender once they have been chopped. Use only very ripe, very delicious mangoes.

2. Then pour three tbsp of sugar into the blender or food processor. Mangoes vary widely in sweetness, so adjust the amount of sugar applied accordingly.

3. Mix and process until uniform. Putting aside.

4. Preparing Agar Agar

5. Put two tsp of the chopped agar strands into a small saucepan. You should use scissors to cut the strands as short as you can. It is tough to disintegrate long threads. Blend in a little more than a third of a cup of water.

6. Don't raise the temperature of the pan over medium.

7. Warm this agar and water combination very slowly. The mixture must be stirred at regular intervals.

8. A boil must be revered in the solution. Be sure the strands are completely dissolved in the water by continuing to stir the mixture as it boils.

9. Once the filaments have broken down in the water, a clear, jelly- like substance will emerge.

10. After waiting 20 seconds, add the agar solution to the jar of mango puree. Agar agar solution should be scraped from the sides and added.

11. Put in three-quarters of a cup of coconut milk. Re-blend until the mixture is uniform.

12. Transfer the pudding to serving dishes. Use a spatula to level out the pudding's top layer. Use a cover or wrap the bowls in aluminum foil to keep the food fresh. Allow the pudding to be set in the fridge for at least four hours, preferably overnight.

13. Mango pudding is a delicious delicacy that is best served cold. Add some berries, dried fruits, or cubed mango just before serving.

CHINESE ALMOND COOKIES

Prep time: 20 minutes

Cook time: 15 minutes

Ingredients

- 1 1/3 cups of almond flour, lightly packed
- 1 cup of (2 sticks) unsalted butter, chilled and cut into cubes
- Pinch kosher salt
- 2 large eggs, divided
- 1 tsp almond extract
- 1 3/4 cups of all-purpose flour
- 1 cup of plus
- 2 tbsp sugar
- 1/2 tsp baking soda
- Thinly sliced almonds, for decoration

Method

1. Mix the almond flour, salt, and butter in the bowl of an electric mixer fitted with the paddle attachment. Beat the ingredient on medium speed for 3 minutes. There will be a noticeable increase in the mixture's coarseness and chunkiness.

2. Mix with an egg and the essence of almonds:

3. Be sure to blend them in at a moderate speed until they are completely absorbed.

4. Throw in some sugar, flour, and baking soda.

5. To incorporate the flour, sugar, and baking soda, sift them before adding them. Slowly mix the ingredients.

6. Put the dough in the fridge by shaping it into a disc and wrapping it in plastic. You should chill it in the fridge for at least two hours.

7. Start by preheating the oven and preparing the baking sheet:

8. Turn on the oven to 325degree Fahrenheit. Put some parchment paper on a baking pan.

9. The last egg should be beaten:

10. Whisk the remaining egg in a separate dish.

11. Roll the dough into 3/4-inch-wide balls and then flatten them on the baking sheet. Put them on the sheet so that they are about an inch apart, and then push your hand down on them so that they form a coin.

12. Place the slivered almonds where you want them and use the egg to decorate the biscuits.

13. Indent the middle of every cookie with a single almond that has been dipped in silver. Finally, decorate every cookie with the egg using a pastry brush or your finger. After baking, the cookie will have a glossy finish. Thanks this.

14. Baking: Preheat the oven to 325 degrees Fahrenheit, then bake for 13 to 15 minutes or until the sides are lightly browned. Put the sheet with the cooling rack in the refrigerator.

CHINESE DOUGHNUT STICKS

Prep: 20 minutes

Cook: 15 minutes

Ingredients

- 400g all-purpose flour/plain flour
- 2 tsp baking powder
- ¼ tsp baking soda, optional
- ½ tsp salt
- 2 eggs, lightly beaten, plus water mixed to 250g
- 2 tbsp neutral cooking oil, plus a little for coating

Instructions

1. The high moisture content of this dough makes it quite finicky to work with. But don't give up hope; I have some advice that should assist.

2. If you have a stand mixer, you may use it to mix and knead the dough for about 8 minutes on low speed. Remove it from the bowl by rubbing oil on your hands.

3. If making by hand, mix all the ingredients with a silicon spatular until you get a dough that looks a little rough. Wrap up and have a 15-minute nap. Spread some oil on your hands. A fist works well for pressing the dough. Then fold it in half, fingertip to fingertip, from the side to the middle. Keep doing this until the dough is completely smooth.

4. To make two equal portions, cut the dough in half. Then, roll them into two even balls with your hands (oiling them if necessary). Spread oil all over them. Wrap with cling wrap and take a nap.

5. Since this is breakfast food, you may wish to wait until the morning to cook the dough, so you have the option of letting it rise at room temperature (for 2 to 4 hours) or in the refrigerator (for 12 to 16 hours). If the

latter, then the dough should be brought back to room temperature before frying. The intended expansion won't occur otherwise.

6. At this point, the dough should be quite pliable and easy to work with. Place them on a floured surface gently (don't knead again). Make two rectangles (every about 10 by 25 centimeters or 4 by 10 inches) by molding them with your hands.

7. Press a ball of dough out with your fingers.

8. Sprinkle a little flour over the top of the dough. Then, divide every rectangle in half horizontally to create 10 equal strips (use a long, sharp knife to make it neat).

9. Stack the dough strips up against every other. Stick them together by pressing the center with a chopstick. Use the remaining bits of dough in the same way.

10. Since it takes time for the deep-frying oil to every the proper temperature, you should begin heating it while you shape the dough.

11. When the oil thermometer reads 190 degrees Celsius (374 degrees Fahrenheit), reduce the heat to low. Carefully stretch the dough and lower it into the oil, taking care to avoid splattering (be careful not to splash).

12. In a matter of seconds, the dough will rise to the top. Keep rolling it with the chopsticks. When it has finished browning evenly and has stopped puffing, move it to a platter lined with paper towels (to soak up excess oil).

13. To finish cooking the remaining dough, just repeat the previous steps. Two sticks may be fried at the same time without lowering the oil temperature too much.